The Song of the Spinning Sun

A true story

MARY FRANCES

AuthorHouse™ UK Ltd.
500 Avebury Boulevard
Central Milton Keynes, MK9 2BE
www.authorhouse.co.uk
Phone: 08001974150

First published by Trafford 2007

Published by AuthorHouse 10/22/2009

ISBN: 978-1-4490-3318-7 (sc)

This book is printed on acid-free paper.

This book is dedicated with my everlasting thanks to my sister Norah who has been my most generous and enthusiastic backer; to my sister Paddy, who told me years ago to practise my writing; to my sister Kathleen for her unflagging prayer power; to my son John for his consistent support through all the bad times, to my parents for giving me a love of music and words and to my ex-husband Geoffrey, for teaching me how to use and value them.

So many people have had a share in my SONG - the friends who came with me (and rescued me from time to time), the doubters who thought I was having a mid-life crisis, and both my wonderful, remarkable sons, Gerard and John, who watched it all with a sort of bemused curiosity.

I am also eternally grateful to Fr Gerry Walsh of St Joseph's parish for his encouragement, and to Aubrey Mitchell, Cliff Mallinson and Bill Barna for their patient and long-suffering (and vital) help and advice with digital technology.

So many others have supported me that to thank them all individually would be impossible, but without Zan Ferris, Cathy Butler, Mary and Dominic Meigh, Anne Dube, John Steward, Dot Brozaitis, Pat Boucousis, Margaret Bush, Jane Rees, Mary Gilmartin and Lorna Davies, the book could not have set out on its journey at all.

As for the rest - *they know who they are! And I salute them.*

INTRODUCTION

There is no real beginning to a life-changing event. One can go back and back, tracing steps, finding causes, according blame. But since a story has to start somewhere, I decided to begin this one immediately before the moment of change itself.

To be precise I went from total unbelief in God to total belief in about 30 seconds.

Life, however, is not composed of straight lines, clear roads and readable signposts. Most of us muddle along following maps with bits missing, or with no maps at all. Sometimes, though, a signpost is lit up like a star, a neon, brilliant and insistent - in which case all one can do is follow it.

On 23rd April 1978 I was presented with my neon star. There was even a map to go with it. So I followed both.

Nothing in the years since then has caused me to change my mind. In fact, all the good, bad, ugly or spectacular events that followed that day in April have merely confirmed my decision. Truth, when you find it, is unarguable.

THE SONG OF THE SPINNING SUN is the story of a journey. All stories should really have a beginning, a middle and an end. This one has a beginning and a middle but no end because, as Frodo and Bilbo sing in The Lord Of The Rings, *"The road goes ever on and on.......and I must follow if I can."*

(J R R Tolkien, "The Fellowship Of The Ring)

"And I will raise you up on eagles' wings
Bear you on the breath of dawn
Make you to shine like the sun
And hold you in the palm of my hand".
(Michael Joncas)

CHAPTER ONE

On 23rd April 1978 at about five o'clock, I was a compass influenced by a million distracting metal parts. My needle veered haphazardly, pointing nowhere in particular. But at somewhere around two minutes past five I found the magnetic North.

For many years until then I'd been what one usually called a 'free spirit'. That means of course that I'd shuffled off 30-odd years of traditional Roman Catholic upbringing and had resolved, one historic day in the middle of Mass, that from then on nobody would ever again Tell Me What To Believe. I'd had enough, I thought, of being brainwashed by holy priests and holy nuns and traditions that went back to Methuselah (or, in this case of course, to Moses!)

So I was a free-thinker. Unfortunately that didn't make me as open-minded as it should have done, since a massive chunk of this free thought, disagreeably labelled 'Religion', had been thrown out of my equations altogether and was not at all likely to creep back in. That is, not if I had anything to do with it.

But at two minutes past five o'clock there I was in a very large convent chapel, standing against a wall because the place was so full of people there was nowhere to sit. My two sisters and my friend Amelia were with me, my sister Norah, in deference to her arthritic hip, taking the only available seat, and we were part of a large, pressed throng. There seemed to be almost as many standing up as sitting down.

I had begun the day as a hostile non-participant but had spent several hours undergoing certain changes of outlook. However, had anyone told me a few days earlier that I would find myself in a chapel at all, let alone standing up in one for an entire service, I wouldn't have stayed around to check this out. Certainly not. I was free.

The previous week had been characteristically busy. Well, frenetic actually. This, however, was nothing new. I was working my last-but-one week as secretary to an Insurance broker. My car had failed its MOT. Every evening was filled. On Thursday there had been a hen party for a friend and on Friday there was a concert at Bristol's Colston Hall at which I was to sing a small solo part.

By Friday morning I finally realised it was all quite impossible. As usual, I had over-reached myself. Owing to the fact that her mother lived on the other side of the country, the hen-party bride had chosen my house to be married from, which meant the imminent invasion early next morning by herself, her father and three bridesmaids. Some house cleaning was therefore necessary. My car had to be fetched from the garage where it was being repaired and re-tested, requiring a bus ride across town in the rush hour, and I was already very, very tired.

So I rang a friend and asked her to sing my solo piece at the Colston Hall that evening.

That's such an easy thing to say, yet how momentous it really was. Non-singers, unaware of the inwardness and exigencies of amateur operatic societies, might think giving up a solo part in that kind of situation quite sensible and realistic. Not worth a second thought. But voluntarily throwing away a moment of minor stardom, standing up in front of an audience of a thousand or more in a prestigious building, is not done casually – if at all! The show must go on, mustn't it? So one has to be very tired indeed or else indifferent to normal human values. After all, vanity is vanity, and my human values were (still are) definitely alive and kicking. So although I was bone and brain weary it was still definitely a sacrifice.

My soprano friend was shocked at the request but went on to sing my part all the same and, as it turned out, I never had the chance to redeem my reputation. But it was either that or my friend's wedding. I simply hadn’t the stamina for both. And one can hardly ask a bride to postpone the happiest day of her life while one of the guests (however important) gets her breath back. So I gave up a last chance of stardom and, apart from my substitute, I don't suppose anyone really noticed.

On Saturday morning we were invaded, as expected. The bride, her father and the bridesmaids all arrived at a nice early hour, as arranged. What was not expected (but of course should have been if I'd had any wits left) was the additional presence of the bride's mother. To be honest, I had forgotten all about her, since up to then she had played no part at all in the proceedings and hadn't even been mentioned. Also unanticipated was an extra body in the person of the littlest bridesmaid's mother, Jackie.

We only had one small spare bedroom and by this time there were rather too many people to go in it.

I had, however, organised my morning with military precision to the last second. I knew exactly what had to be done and when I was going to do it. Unfortunately this state of affairs was abruptly changed by the bride, who thrust into my unsuspecting hand an expensive white veil, a headdress and a photograph.

"Can you sew that on like that?" she asked cheerfully, and departed.

A truthful, if hard-hearted, answer would have been no, I couldn't, but in this case the question was obviously rhetorical. So, in a moment of resignation which turned rapidly into despair, I delegated as many of my own jobs as I could to my husband and my friend Amelia, who had come to house-and-cat-sit while we were out, immured myself silently in our master bedroom, as alone as I could possibly make myself, and sat down to work the puzzle out.

It turned out to be impossible to solve and I'm not sure even now what went onto the bride's head. I certainly did nothing else at all that morning, and events took place in the rest of the house which I shall doubtless never know about. But finally we all stood on the landing, the bride, her parents and me, trying to pin into place a not entirely completed head-dress and trying to be calm.

I was calmest of all. So calm, in fact, that nobody – least of all me – recognised the true state of things. The veil and the unworkable photograph, coming on top of a week of impossibly crammed arrangements, had pushed me into a new state altogether. I'd been tired before. I was now catatonic. There was, however, no chance to do anything about it because the wedding was overdue and the bride was late.

We left Amelia behind as caretaker, which was just as well since our final departure was so hasty that the bride went without her bouquet and Amelia, wearing jeans and a sweater, had to chase the procession into the next-door car park crying "Stop, stop!" The very handsome vintage Bentley, hired for the morning and completely open to the weather, was surrounded by admirers and interested local shoppers, all waiting to see the bride drive off in a high wind. The sudden eruption of Amelia flourishing a bouquet no doubt added greatly to the fun.

Our own little yellow Daf was parked in our drive, which is hard to negotiate even when not in a hurry, so by the time we had emerged into the road the Bentley had started up and vanished into the traffic. My husband sat next to me in the passenger seat (courtesy of his long legs), while the littlest bridesmaid's mother squeezed herself into the tiny, cramped rear seat. A Daf coupé is a sports model with a sloping back. Adults definitely not catered for.

I was sorry for her, not only because she was forced to keep her head twisted in order to avoid scraping it along the car roof, but because she'd been obliged to wait for us until the rest of the procession – including her small daughter – had departed. When we lost sight of the Bentley she must have known there was a good chance of missing the enchanting sight of her daughter tripping daintily up the aisle in a charming Victorian dress with long frilly pantaloons and a poke bonnet. Jackie was, however, serene and soothing and smelt delicious. As I turned the corner, having mislaid the bride and realising we were now in for a race in Saturday traffic right through the centre of the city, I commented on the perfume and, with that plunging sense of catastrophe which tells us we've left the gas on, I knew I'd forgotten my own perfume.

I like perfume. I like wearing it. And now I was filled with such an urgent sense of loss that I cried out in anguish and Jackie leaned forward (not easy in our Daf) and offered me some of her own. I can't smell ‘Charlie’ now without remembering the day and the car ride and the rush. Most of all it reminds me of Jackie. We only met once more, years later, but it would be nice to see her again one day. I would buy her a bottle of ‘Charlie’.

The drive through Bristol had a dreamlike quality, the sort of dream where traffic lights are always red and heavy lorries grow monstrously huge and fill up the road in front, where pedestrians are mysteriously impelled to suicide and all other traffic lanes are invariably emptier than the one you happen to be in.

There was also a new, and until then unrecognised, problem. I didn't know the way. Never having been to this particular church before, I had naively assumed we'd be following the bridal car and had therefore neglected to find the place on my A-Z guide. But I wasn't especially worried. So long as I drove towards the correct corner of Bristol the church would, I felt, materialise – so I gave a few general directions to my husband, left him to navigate and drove doggedly on.

Unfortunately, the stress of the day brought on one of our periodic breakdowns in transmission and we found ourselves in one of those familiar, bewildering arguments in which I collapse into total incoherence. We were both right. We were simply not communicating. The road we were looking for was Southmead Road, and this I knew approximately where to find. But Southmead Road is one of those irritating ones which change their names half way along, so when I turned a corner into a road called something quite different my husband most sensibly pointed that we were going the wrong way. My reply was incomprehensible. Too exhausted to press the correct button on my computer brain, my thoughts refused point blank to be forced into any recognisable pattern. The result was gibberish. We therefore drove the rest of the way in silence.

I shall never know how we eventually found the right church. But unbelievably there it was, and there was the bride waiting for us with her worried-looking entourage. She and her veil had come through the equivalent of a force nine hurricane sitting in the very high seat of a very open car, and with a brief flicker of compassion (not untinged with amusement), I thought of all her anxious combings in front of our bedroom mirror. I gave the veil a brief glance to assess possible damage, decided it was as right as it was ever likely to be, and passed through into the church, to sit with my husband inconspicuously at the back.

My hat, chosen for its elegance and unquestionably the nicest hat I'd ever possessed, was however a mite too big and either moved spontaneously around on my head or, whenever I looked right or left, stayed obstinately where it was. Moreover I was hot and flushed and uncomfortably aware of how late we all were.

The wedding itself, though apparently just a prelude to what was to come next day (a fact of which I was not the least bit aware and wouldn't have appreciated even if I had been) was, however, an essential part of the experience. It started a new train of thought.

Getting married in front of us were a divorced man and a young girl, and it was all taking part in an Anglican church. They had had to search hard to find a vicar prepared to perform this ceremony. It was also, in its way, a hugely fashionable affair. The world and its trimmings were very much on display. So as I sat, utterly weary, wearing a wilfully rebellious hat and conditioned by years both in and out of the church, I was conscious of some new thought processes. If they meant what they were saying, I felt, then they should not be saying it.

"Till death us do part," the bridegroom said. "Forsaking all others," he said.

Does one believe in God? I thought. Do they? Does the bridegroom? If not, why go to all this trouble, through all this meaningless rigmarole, just to fulfil a social requirement? Was it merely a tribal custom, like the horse shoes and confetti? If so, why make a promise to God if there wasn't one?

On the other hand, if one did believe in God, how could one make the same promise twice?

Obscurely disturbed, I sang the hymns and listened to the address and the readings, and eventually joined the rest of the guests outside for the photographs, curiously unmoved by the sight of the bride's head-dress coming unsewn over one ear. A tiny stirring of sympathy eventually made me reach out a hand to try and tuck it back, but the world had suddenly become too big for minutiae like recalcitrant wedding veils.

The reception was large and lavish, in a hotel that smelt of carpets and luxury and which seemed to have no windows, for daylight was shut out and we were enclosed in a soft-smelling, padded igloo. Geoffrey and I, having lost Jackie and knowing no-one else, sat at a table with strangers. My next-door neighbour devoted himself entirely to the voluptuously attractive young woman on his other side. The food was magnificent. There were mountains of ham, lobster, salmon and a whole boar's head complete with tusks carried in by a procession of white-coated waiters. I found myself feeling sorry for the boar, and didn't eat any. Fresh cream desserts overflowed into gateaux and trifles and we drank champagne. Speeches and telegrams were followed by the presentation of bouquets to the two mothers and public thanks to everyone – everyone, that is except me.

I sat with my husband at our obscure table, thinking back over the morning and my labours over the clean, flower-bedecked house and the unworkable veil, but although surprised and hurt when the thanks didn't come, I was almost too tired to care.

As usual Geoffrey and I were bored and lonely in the company of so many people with whom we seemed to have so little in common. A few years earlier I would probably have made an effort, talking resolutely to strangers and persuading myself, with a natural talent for self deception, that I was having fun.

But today I could do neither. Weary of socialising and bored with the questionable pleasure of Doing Up The Bridegroom's Car ("Don't be silly, they expect it – they'd be disappointed if we didn't"), we said goodbye and left for home, battered into a sort of dazed silence.

Amelia was waiting for us. The house was bright and cool and polished, and there were flowers and open windows and sunshine on the carpet. We had tea and cakes on the floor, sharing the sunshine with the cat.

Amelia and I were going out again. My son was to play the drums with a quartet called 'Sahaja' and Amelia was afraid of looking shabby and inelegant. I wasn't. I knew where we were going.

CHAPTER TWO

Bristol's Dockland Settlement is nowhere near the docks. I haven't been there recently, but in 1978 it was an apparently uncared for building in the heart of the inner city. Even then it had a doubtful reputation, but it later became notorious because of terrible unemployment and the racial rioting that swept the country. At the time, though, we felt safe enough. When I asked John whether I could walk there at night, he had actually been amused.

"The only thing you might get," he said "is being mistaken for someone else", a comment I was not sure was entirely complimentary, but when Amelia and I arrived that evening I understood. Inside the building the students and the bearded teachers and the girls in granny-print dresses were welcoming and unsuspicious. We couldn't have been safer.

We sat, the two of us, in a darkish room where the wall surfaces seemed mostly undecorated, half-plastered and in some cases, so far as I could determine in the dim light, merely uncovered brick. The bar was functional but the service quick and the face of the bartender friendly and pleasant. In trousers and an old jacket I felt more at ease than at any moment during the day – more at home than in the luxurious igloo of a hotel or in the crowded church with the behatted ladies and the hymn books and the equivocal vows.

Sahaja was good, but then Sahaja was always good. There were two guitars, a violin and a set of hand drums. The music, a touch of rock, a whiff of oriental and a hint of jazz, was not entirely to my taste, but as usual the real point of the evening was the sight and sound of John, brilliant on the hand drums – so compelling in what he was doing that the fact of his being my son was simply an extra bonus.

He took little notice of me, but that didn't matter. Pre-concert nerves tend to make us all too pre-occupied for social niceties and I knew too much about them not to sympathise with his. He was a tad dishevelled, not as clean as he might have been, and he wasn't wearing his glasses. But he was happy and I hadn't seen him for a week or two so he could have appeared in a plastic bag or a mud pack for all I cared.

After the performance the audience applauded with energy and enthusiasm. I bought John a drink and he peered short-sightedly at me over the top of it and introduced me to a friend, whose name I forgot at once. So far as I know I haven't met him since, but I do remember that he was politely charming and seemed quite happy talking to the drummer's mother. I was dimly conscious of Amelia on the outer limits; of a game of indoor football being played nearby; of the lack of light or comfort, the smoke and dusty, drink-spilled floor and the sound of loud music from the next room. All these elements merged themselves into the indigestible mixture which had been my day and my week. I thought of the large and imposing concert I'd sacrificed the night before, at which I could have stood on a famous stage with a full choir of tenors, altos, sopranos and basses. I thought of the insurance broker whose office I was to leave the very next week, with little regret I have to confess. I thought of the despoiling of my carefully planned morning with all its consequences, of the lavishly unreal wedding reception and the even less convincing church ceremony that preceded it.

This, I thought, was more real to me than any of them. This basic place, stripped of trimmings, where playing the hand drums in a dim hall meant exactly that and no more. I knew, of course, that it wasn't my own sort of basic life and that the general lack of comfort was really only acceptable because I could leave it again whenever I chose; that among these people would be the junkies and pot-smokers, the neurotics of their generation, and that all of them would have their own pretensions – if not to hats and sybaritic hotel lounges at least to hard benches and beer-slopped bars. But John was my focal point that evening and he, as always, was neither more nor less than John.

When the time came I found it hard to leave the company of people who appeared to accept us for what we were, without question, and who asked nothing except that we did the same for them.

As soon as we arrived home Amelia and I went straight to bed. There was to be an early start next day.

At this point it is now necessary to pause, as the events of the weekend so far had been no more than curtain raisers for Act One of a new drama. Important curtain raisers for they set the scene and established an attitude of mind, but the day which followed held a significance almost beyond my power to describe, either then or since. Even now, after all these years, I have to take the description a step at a time, for although the central core of it was simple, the circumstances surrounding it were not.

We awoke to find the morning fresh, clear and light. We ate toast and drank coffee and said goodbye to Geoffrey and I strapped Amelia into the passenger seat of our little primrose yellow coupe, but there was no place in my conscious thought for anything except that ahead of me was a ninety mile drive up the motorway to Birmingham, with another ninety miles back again next morning. We were to stay with my sister in her little town house in Moseley, so we had our overnight cases and should have been in holiday spirit.

My spirit was, it seemed, anaesthetised. I didn't care where we were going or why.

We were in fact on our way to something called a Day Of Renewal at a Birmingham convent, but my role was simply that of chauffeuse. Amelia wanted to go, so I was driving her there. All very simple. When I thought about the day at all, it was to look forward to a period of quiet peace, where I could unhook all the stresses of daily life and float free in comfortable nothingness.

Having rid myself of religion forever, I now felt nothing but a strong urge never again to be cornered or trapped into believing anything against my will or better judgement. I was happy with my open mind. It meant I could explore avenues as they came, treating clairvoyance, astrology, science fiction and psychic phenomena with the same degree of curiosity and tolerance. People who maintained there was nothing beyond this life were, I felt, taking a big risk – not because I believed in anything specific myself but because I thought such rigid views in such an age were dangerous to the point of insanity.

"A hundred years ago," I said one day to a middle aged man who seemed amused by my lively and disrespectful opinions. "A hundred years ago, if someone had told you could watch live people on the other side of the world doing things right now this minute on a television screen, or tried to describe an ipod or a mobile phone, you'd have told them they were talking absolute rubbish. And you'd have been wrong"

"I only believe what I can touch and prove"

I had laughed. "But a hundred years ago you couldn't have touched a TV set so you wouldn't have believed it. Anyway, if ten people hold different views about death, nine of them are going to be surprised aren't they? And the number could be a thousand, not ten, which would make you the thousandth, with nine hundred and ninety nine being surprised. But even if you only had a 50% chance of being right, would you trust yourself on a plane if you thought it had a 50% chance of crashing?"

My friend had smiled tolerantly, indifferent to my childish arguments, but I had been serious. How arrogant he was, I thought.

Finally he said, firmly with no room whatsoever for doubt or further discussion "When you die you're dead", and I gave up, thinking privately that one day one of us was indeed going to be surprised.

It wasn't what I personally believed, though, that was in question, for I didn't really know what I believed. I was content to wait and see – if necessary until after death. In other ways, however, I was not at all content and had been growing less and less content as years went by, less and less inclined to enjoy what I had and more and more inclined to find fault, to criticise and regret lost chances. I felt somehow purposeless and needed the carrot of nice things to look forward to. A weekend away, a party to plan, a holiday, anything at all as a point of reference to give excitement and purpose to what seemed more and more a task of getting through the days.

So when my sister Norah came to stay with us a year earlier, telling us about marvellous new happenings in the Catholic Church, I wasn't very impressed. If she spoke about healing I said faith healers claimed to do that. When she described testimonies and spontaneous prayer and singing, I told her that sort of thing had been going on for years at Pentecostal and Baptist revival meetings.

I side-stepped every attempt on her part to entice me to Birmingham for one of her jamboree Sundays. I said it all sounded interesting, then (I hope politely) presented my excuses. Norah had always been a traditional cradle Catholic, but in my opinion at that time (I've learnt better since!) had always been suggestible and emotional. I had no intention of being either.

She told me that our elder sister, Kathleen, had also shown interest in these goings on. I admit this sent the first flicker of curiosity into my antagonistic brain because Kathleen had been a nun for almost my entire life. She had entered her convent at the age of 18, when I was merely three, but despite spending 40 years as a Holy Sister, Kathleen (official name Sister Angela) had always seemed sensible and not given to sudden enthusiasms, especially not to such questionable ones as those I was hearing about.

Then my friend Amelia went to South Africa to stay with her daughter. This particular daughter had lived a strenuous, incident-packed life which she had described in a highly autobiographical novel. Since I had typed this novel fairly recently, I felt I knew a fair amount about the girl and was therefore amazed when Amelia had received a new white Bible from her daughter with a note that her next novel "had been still-born because she was too busy being converted". Amelia duly left for South Africa and was away for several weeks.

She came home in a strange state of mind which she tried to communicate but couldn't. She was, she said, "a newly hatched chicken running around all wet". And although I recognised the description I didn't understand the reason for it. Why was she a newly hatched chicken?

Very hesitantly, like Norah, she explained that she'd encountered something inexpressible. Healings, prophecies and testimonies were all touched on, but mostly she talked about the change in herself.

By this time I was becoming both irritated and reluctantly curious. Amelia was an Anglican and the phenomena she was describing in an Anglican community in South Africa were identical to the phenomena Norah was describing in a Roman Catholic community in Birmingham. So, while privately filing the information for future use, publicly I said nothing. Putting my head into such a risky boiling pot was something I had absolutely no intention of doing.

Instead I contented myself with trying to save Amelia from despair. She was obviously suffering. I didn't take this too seriously, as she was at the time an intense little person. A matter of agony for her might simply be an irritation to lesser mortals, yet all the same her loneliness and deprivation were both extreme and puzzling.

"It was the most exciting and fulfilling experience I've ever known," she told me "and I'm missing it". So we set about trying to find it in Bristol – without success I have to admit. Certainly it didn't seem to be at her beautiful and rather High Anglican church in the heart of Bristol where she'd been a faithful and devout worshipper for years. So in a spirit of research, and with Norah's tales in mind, I decided to try a Roman Catholic church instead, and phoned the priest at a church not far away, to ask him for a Mass prayer book. After all, her new ‘something’ could as well be there as anywhere.

I went off to collect the prayer book and decided I liked the priest's face. He was tiny but dignified, and his expression managed in some inexplicable way to be both human and spiritual at the same time. I felt he was trustworthy and made a mental note of this, for although it was highly unlikely I'd ever need his help, I've always liked to hedge my bets!

Amelia and I went to Mass the following Sunday, but although the service was serene and pleasant, her ‘something’ wasn't there either so we didn't go again.

Some weeks later Norah phoned from Moseley to say there was to be a Day of Renewal on April 23rd and would I like to go. By this time I was beginning to give up trying to help Amelia in her quest, mostly because I couldn't understand the reason for it – or for our lack of success – and so I surrendered. Norah I could withstand, but not Norah and Amelia at the same time.

"What you're looking for," I told my forlorn-looking friend, "seems to be up in Birmingham, so we'd better go".

She was delighted, but I forgot about it at once. There were too many other things going on in my life. Besides, it was something I didn’t care to think about, being to do with ‘Religion’ and therefore suspect. So I filed it away in a dark corner of my subconscious under ‘things to do after the wedding’. A day out in Birmingham was just an additional hurdle at the end of a week of hurdles.

Thus, as we drove up the M5 on this sunny Sunday morning, I was thinking of nothing at all. I was as empty and motiveless as the vase on my windowsill, except for a desire to arrive at our destination as uneventfully as possible.

This was my day out. Out of commission, out of mind, in neutral.

CHAPTER THREE

We arrived at Norah's house to find her buttering small piles of assorted sandwiches. My sister loves feeding people. She was especially excited about where we were going and as she cut and spread she talked about who we'd see and what might happen. "The music! The music and the singing! Oh Mary, it's so lovely you'll cry".

With this I was quite prepared to agree. Music is the key to my emotions. Some pieces I can't hear without having a vital button pressed somewhere in the region of my solar plexus, leaving me sobbing passionately into whatever, or whoever, is at hand. So I accepted the warning and a packet of Norah's tissues, and prepared myself. Not without misgivings. I intended to keep as detached and calm as possible, since it was clear that tiredness alone would undo me eventually, and I wanted to keep out of trouble during this particular day if I could.

After breakfast we drove to Selly Park Convent and stepped out into bright, strong sunlight. Among the first people I saw was our sister Kathleen, wearing her navy dress and short veil. Although her name in the convent is not Kathleen but Angela, neither Norah nor I have been able to change the habit of years. She was pleased to see me but was wise enough to keep her enthusiasm in check, since I was obviously feeling cool about the whole thing. There were other nuns there too from other convents, but I was not aware enough to notice anything except generalised impressions, smells, the feel of the path under my shoes, human beings on all sides.

The large conference hall was carpeted and comfortable. Sunshine sent bars of light onto rows of chairs. Companionable conversation fell like the sunshine, filtering and permeating the room with its own warmth. There was an impressive number of people, with more coming through the door all the time, and they were all smiling. For some reason this annoyed me.

We found seats near the front, all in one row. I sat between Amelia and Norah and looked with faint distaste at the song sheets waiting on my chair. The stage was decorated with a banner saying "Life in the Spirit", and underneath it were some chairs with four guitars propped against them. As the room grew fuller the owners of the guitars climbed onto the stage and took up their instruments, strapping them on and tuning them. They were all young.

I don't remember much about how everything began, except that eventually the hall was filled to the corners. An elderly nun sitting behind me leaned forward to ask if I had ever been to one of these things before. I said no, I hadn't. "They're all different," she said, happily puzzled. "Every meeting is different from every other meeting, but there's nothing to worry about, so don't be alarmed".

I promised not to be alarmed, having never suspected I might be, and was only mildly curious about why she felt any warning was necessary. Disturbance of spirit, in any form whatsoever, was not part of my plan for the day.

The guitarists began to play and we were asked to sing something from the printed sheets, and suddenly there everyone was, joining in. The songs were cheerful, lively, lusty and melodic. While not exactly on the highest level of musical excellence, they were easy to learn, with a strong beat and a vitality that annoyed me. The beat I liked, but the vitality I definitely did not. It had a basic, unsophisticated quality which I found banal, the stuff for children.

The songs were all too easy. I decided not to sing. Anyway I was too tired. Once or twice my mouth opened of its own accord and a pathetic squeak emerged, always strangled at first croak.

Something in the region of stomach level was telling me very positively to be quiet.

After some time of this non-singing, I looked around briefly and quickly, not wanting to be caught staring. I found myself surrounded by an unfamiliar element. And I was suddenly, vehemently and totally angry. "How dare they?" I thought, "How dare they look so happy?"

For what I saw was more than enthusiasm, more than just a lot of people enjoying themselves. It was a simple, uninhibited and entirely unfashionable happiness.

Furious, I turned back to face the stage and the guitars. "They are all so smug," I told myself, "sitting here singing these awful, silly, stupid songs. They're all so complacent and I hate them"

Then I burst into tears.

Even then I realised that the events of the week were bound to overtake me sooner or later. There are limits, after all, to human resilience and, as I knew perfectly well, too much stress in my case inevitably ends in tears, so I reached into my handbag for the bottle of tranquillisers which permanently nestled there, and took one. Norah saw but said nothing. Then, fortified, I sat still and silent, hoping as always that the threat of humiliating public tears would go away and leave me alone. But the songs were too joyful and I had had enough. Within seconds I was sobbing, my face in my hands and all hope of control gone, it seemed, forever.

Amazingly, nobody took any notice. I was allowed to sob myself into a kind of numb quietness and acknowledge what had been patently obvious ever since that fatal glance behind me. I was the only unhappy person in the room. And a loneliness so vast and encompassing filled me that a deep silence took the place of tears. It seemed that my entire life had been spent in some kind of isolation, sometimes out of choice to pursue my own fantasy life, but often because somehow I never quite fitted the required mould. The wedding, the reception, even John's gig, had as usual left me like a small moon encircling the globe of other peoples' closeness, for in this isolation I had learned to be sociable. A Party Girl, the life and soul of assemblies, the one who flirted and made easy friendships. 'Jokey Mary'

Hardly any of this was precisely formulated as I sat in the Selly Park conference hall, and some of it I was aware of only as one is aware of distant traffic sounds, but hundreds of people surrounded me with their happiness and I had become fiercely conscious of my own exclusion from it. The realisation was sharp and clear but I wasn't sure what I wanted to do about it. Once again I was a moon encircling an unfamiliar sun, though this time it was a sun I couldn't immediately identify. I only knew it was warm and inexpressibly attractive, yet I was not convinced I wanted to be a part of it. The other side of the coin of isolation is dependence. Is it possible to have the one without paying the price of the other? Had I not always resisted this seductive closeness simply because I had to stay free?

There was a priest in charge of the proceedings, on the stage with the guitarists. Until then I'd been too absorbed in my own feelings to notice him, but now, with the sort of muzzy attention of someone emerging from an afternoon nap, I began to take him in.

He was asking us all to praise God in a murmur of sound. A strange thing to do, I thought, and surely contrived? But I had gone with no preconceived ideas, so everything was new and this request no more alien than anything else in this alien place. The murmur which came in response remained quiet and restrained, a murmur and no more, and I didn't know then that some people might have expected more. In the corners of my memory were images of Pentecostal gatherings where people shouted "Hallelujah!" and Praise the Lord!" but I wasn't relating this particular day with Pentecostal or any other kind of religious behaviour – noisy or otherwise. I simply hadn't thought about it. So when this ripple of sound lapped about me in small, warm waves, I was interested and watchful but nothing more. I think I was mostly watching for signs of stage-management.

Apart from the musicians, a man and woman on stage were obviously in control though in an unstructured kind of way. It seemed to me they didn't determine what was happening but just kept a finger on the general pulse – less perhaps to influence it than to keep it from over-influencing itself. At one point a man in his forties came from the back of the hall to sit on the stage steps. There were tears on his cheeks. Someone gave him a microphone and laid a hand on his shoulder.

"When I came today," he said, "I thought that praising God was just an emotional gimmick, whipped up emotion and hysteria. But when Father asked us to praise God just now, for the first time in my life I found myself really praising him. I mean really, really praising him. I just wanted you to know". Then he stood up and went back down the hall.

That man, with the unhysterical tears and quiet English voice was one of the many impressions to be made on me that day. I will never know who he was. Perhaps if he reads this he might recognise himself.

Lunch was a noisy, friendly business. Huge pots of tea stood on long tables. There were plates of sandwiches and rolls. We had taken our own, but as everyone seemed to be eating everyone else's, we did the same. My tranquillisers had begun to take effect so I was behaving more normally, enjoying the tea and conversation though not participating except in a general way, and with only the surface of my mind. I was still very quiet, but content now to drift with the day and let it take me where it would.

That tranquilliser was the last I would ever take.

When the last crumb had been eaten and the last drop of tea poured from the monster pots, we wandered back to the conference hall to hear a testimony. This time I sat at the back. I wanted to think and needed to be alone to do it. The girl on stage was young and she told her story quietly and calmly. She seemed to have a personal awareness of God that was new to me. She lived in a shared house with three others like herself and they had a room set aside for a chapel. She also talked about seminars in a way that assumed everyone present knew what they were.

Her story left me unmoved but interested in what she had to say, and curious about the idea of a personal relationship with God. He was obviously a real person to her.

Afterwards I found Norah and followed her into one the smaller rooms where she introduced me to her friend Betty. Betty herself had given a testimony only a month or so before. She had had dramatic experiences of God, of his closeness and his reality. She was slim and fashionable, with elegantly tossed red curls, careful make-up and outrageously high heeled shoes. Somehow these facts, while I appreciated them for what they were, confused me because they didn't seem to be in the approved religious mould. Not that I was complaining. If anything I found her appearance both challenging and reassuring.

The trouble was that as soon as she looked at me I felt as if someone had switched on a torch inside my head, making me vulnerable and exposed. This woman, with her ginger coiffure and sophisticated shoes, would know me for what I was. A sham and a fraud!

Norah asked Betty to pray for me. "For her neck" she said, "and for some emotional problems". She didn't specify the problems, but I knew she was thinking of the nervous tic that had plagued me since early teen years. This has since been diagnosed as a mild form of Tourettes Syndrome, but in those days the condition was not generally recognised. Around my neck and across my shoulders, around one eye and down into my cheek, I twitched. Not all the time, of course, and a great deal depended on my mood and who I was with, but most of the time I twitched somewhere or other and nobody at the time had ever succeeded in finding a reason. Several psychiatrists had tried and failed, since apart from the twitch I seemed to be boringly normal. Also in my neck was a small, hard lump which I tended to finger in moments of stress, or deep thought, or boredom or perplexity.

Betty found herself a chair and sat with her hands upturned in her lap. She was praying for me. An hour or so earlier this would have infuriated me. It would have seemed an impertinence, an intrusion. But this afternoon I was intrigued, curious and a trifle nervous. I wondered what would happen.

The room was beginning to fill and a middle-aged couple started answering questions. They were quietly spoken and seemed entirely normal – the usual restrained English middle-class citizens – yet they gave an impression of authority, an unemotional air of conviction which had greater power for me than any dynamic orator. They too talked about seminars, and about what happened when one let the Holy Spirit into one's life. They told their own stories, one undramatic and the other spectacular but both played down and understated. I was impressed, not so much with what they said but how they said it. They were so very British. A far cry from the all-American evangelist.

Then we all walked out into the clean, Spring sunshine and across a garden to the chapel. I was still drifting but calm now and quiet.

"I always love the Mass at these places." Norah said, and Betty replied "Oh yes, it's the best part".

I walked alone, in spirit if not in body, and wondered how the Mass could ever be the best part of anyone's day. I remembered the Masses of my childhood and adolescence, hours of daydreaming while a sexless, depersonalised man in a long coloured robe spoke incomprehensibly in Latin. The familiar routines, smells, colours and the childish sense of warmth and security, even the flowing tones of the Latin I'd learned parrot-fashion and the sense of unalterable tradition had provided a perfect background for my own thoughts and dreams, acting as an unfailing key to them over the years so that certain smells and phrases still let loose the romantic visions of my childhood.

Today the convent chapel was as big as a small church and very crowded. With Norah being persuaded into the only available seat, Kathleen, Amelia and I had to stand against the wall. The guitarists played the same songs we had learned earlier, and by now I was singing along lustily. Over the past few hours my attitude had undergone a series of changes. It may have been the tranquilliser. Whatever it was, I was now a fairly sympathetic, if emotionally detached, observer at an event which I felt was somehow significant – as if I were present at an historic moment, even if it the history being made turned out to be my own.

Ever since my twenties, liturgical ceremonies had always bored me. This one did not. Instead I was finding it aesthetically beautiful. This was no set of routine phrases. A series of actions and poems were being unfurled in a setting of grace and charm and deep meaning.

Then the moment came for what I had always known as Holy Communion. To me this had meant kneeling with one's mouth open at an awkward angle so that a small round wafer could be inserted onto one's tongue. This one must never do with sins on one's conscience, which meant of course that I always felt guilty because no matter how many times I confessed my lapses I always immediately lapsed again, so sins were still always on my conscience. This meant that theoretically I couldn't be in a ‘state of grace’. However, since I had never been very sure what a ‘state of grace’ was, it followed that my felonies were always being compounded at a frightening rate. Was anyone, I thought, ever in this enviable state and, if so, why was I never in it too? The easy solution – the matter of a moment – was to dismiss the whole thing. If there were no God there could be no sin and no state of grace, so my conscience could stay clean and undefiled forever. But even that didn’t work, because even without God I had always possessed a strong sense of fair play, and was invariably overpowered by the knowledge of my own deficiencies.

God or no God, justice alone demanded that one measured up.

Today, however, when this moment for Holy Communion arrived, I surprised myself by making a totally unexpected decision. State of grace or not (and in my case definitely not) I was going to walk up with everyone else to receive it. This decision was not rational or even logical. I simply decided to go.

Amelia nudged me. "Is it all right if I go too?" she asked.

I knew the rules. Amelia was an Anglican, therefore it wasn't 'all right' at all, but I didn't hesitate.

"Who's counting?" I said, nodding at the huge crowd. Privately I added that she was far more deserving than I was but that I wasn't going to let this stop me. So we all filed up together, Norah and Kathleen showing not the smallest flicker of surprise.

After an absence of 12 or so years, it was a weird experience to be handed something as awe-filled and silent as this small round wafer. I watched the people ahead of me and saw them taking it in their cupped hands, so I did the same – relieved that even the act of receiving it was new and different.

There were several priests officiating at the same time, dispersed around the chapel to minister to long queues in different aisles and corners. So many people were filing up that those standing around the walls were asked to leave the chapel altogether to allow space for the ones waiting behind to get back to their own places. So I stood outside the door in a state of calm nothingness, waiting to be re-admitted and feeling no emotion. The quiet serenity of this large crowd was affecting me like a warm bath after an hour in the gym.

At that point a baritone voice was lifted up, quite near to Amelia and me, in a strangely compelling chant. The language was foreign. I wondered if the voice belonged to one of the visiting priests, Spanish perhaps or Italian. The language itself was unfamiliar but washed over me with an odd stirring of peace. I knew it wasn't Latin and I'd never heard this chant before, yet all the same it was suggestive of something I couldn't immediately identify. Then from inside the chapel we heard a murmur, a bit like the sea or the wind in full-leaved trees, which lifted me to a new pitch of wistfulness and longing. Amelia suddenly moved. "I must hear this," she said, "They're singing in tongues".

Despite the fact that I had no idea what she meant, for some reason her words did not surprise me. I didn't know what ‘singing in tongues’ was, but it seemed perfectly in order that whatever it was should be happening at this time and in this place. What else and where else? I thought. So I followed her to the door and brushed past the owner of the baritone voice – no priest but a middle-aged man in ordinary clothes – who sang with his head thrown back and his eyes closed. I glanced at him curiously but no-one else showed any curiosity at all. His voice was strong and confident but quite unaffected. The fact that he was singing seemed utterly natural, in tune with the day and beyond remark.

By the time we had arrived back at our station by the wall, all sound had stopped and there was deep silence. It was a deeper and more filled silence than anything I’d ever known and I was desolate. I'd missed it. Then, very quickly, the thought came that I hadn't deserved to hear it anyway. Such beauty couldn't possibly be for me. If there were a God, how could he love me now?

I was standing lost in resignation when a small voice, piping, isolated, began to sing alone in a far corner. Another joined it and another until there, unbelievably, was the sound I had most wanted to hear but could never have expected or even dared to ask for.

I stood immersed in it. I was in its centre, its core, the heart of an inexpressible, unbearable beauty which billowed softly around me and took my soul and spirit and heart into itself. An all-enveloping harmony sent me swirling and whirling with it like a leaf in the breeze, and with exquisite tenderness whatever is at the centre of myself was lifted into this soft pillar of sound, was touched with radiance and gently returned. And I covered my face and wept.

When I came to myself I was saying "This is it, this is it, this is it", and I knew that in the very heart of it all, within it yet above it, someone had laid a gently compelling finger on me and said "Come on Mary, stop being silly. I want you". And also, even in the act of listening, I recognised that this heart-breaking beauty hadn't been written, orchestrated or rehearsed. There had been no conductor waving a baton. Whoever or whatever had caused it to be, whoever was its source and inspiration, had to be source of all beauty, glory and power. And love.

If this were truly God, then he must be the most perfectly glorious, unutterably breath-taking, wonderful thing I had ever encountered or ever would encounter. "This is it?" This was God, and God was like nothing on earth. He was beauty beyond all imagining.

The rest of the day went by in colourful patches. No-one wanted to go home. We all joined hands and sang "Bind us together" and everyone smiled at me. We encored and encored, clapped and called and begged for more. A very cosmetic lady whose mascara had run down her cheeks and whose elaborate, dyed blonde hair was disentangled on her collar, smiled wryly at me through pink-rimmed eyes.

"It's my first time," she confided, "If anyone had ever told me I wouldn't want to leave after Mass, I wouldn't have believed them. Listen to them all." I listened but was listening inwardly to what was taking place inside my own self. We emerged eventually into the April evening. I was red-eyed and blotchy but no-one said a word. I wanted no conversation, no comment.

We shared a Chinese take-away meal with wine at Norah's house, and I drank the wine very fast, saying nothing and lying silently on the sofa until I went to bed, very early and more than a little drunk. The speed of drinking, the tranquilliser and the events of the day between them sent me instantly to sleep.

I awoke at about two o'clock and lay still. I was filled with the most blissful sense of peace and warmth I had ever known. I was a baby bathed and changed and fed, lying in fragrant safety in her cot. I was a small bird under its mother's wing. I was a cat curled on a sunny cushion. But though I knew something both wonderful and important had happened to me, I didn't really know what it was. I only knew that whatever it might be I must and would have it again, that I must never lose it or be parted from it, and that I would go on searching all my life to find and keep this thing that had so profoundly moved me.

Some time later, still blissfully awake, I raised my fingers to feel the familiar small lump on my neck and found it had gone.

CHAPTER FOUR

I was very quiet all through breakfast, still lost in my night-time peace, and silent on the motorway as I drove Amelia home with the early morning lorries. She talked to me but I never heard or remembered what she said. As we came into Bristol I left her outside her office and drove home. It was my day off, the start of my last week of work for the Insurance Broker. At some point during that morning there was a visit from someone who'd been at the wedding two days before, but who she was and why she'd come was an irrelevance, instantly forgotten. After she left I lay on the spare bed, thinking. What I thought was not clear or concise. It was simply a sort of existing – in new knowledge, in an awareness of something that was wrapping me in stillness.

By lunchtime I realised something must be done. The face of the priest who had lent me the prayer book came back to me as an anchor, a point at which I might just begin to understand this newness, if not cogently than at least in a first tentative step towards cogency. So I looked up his phone number and rang it.

"You won't remember me," I said, "I'm not even in your parish", and I told him something rather strange had just happened to me in Birmingham. "I don't know whether to come and tell you about it now while it's still clear in my head, or let it stew for a week".

Obviously amused, he said he remembered me quite well and I could do whichever I liked.

I didn't hesitate for long. "I'll come now then," I said. While a week might show me whether I'd been affected by emotional exhaustion, it might also make me forget the details, and this I couldn't bear.

"That's right," he agreed. "Come straight away".

Looking back, I am amazed at how much I took for granted. It didn't occur to me for a moment that he wouldn't be interested or even free to see me. This was my day, and of course he would be free.

I went and it was very easy. I was not at all nervous, only intent on sharing an experience I wasn't even sure I could describe. The presbytery was small and bright like the priest himself, who sat diminutive and alert in an armchair in one corner of the tiny reception room while I sat in another. There were bookshelves and a coffee table with leaflets on it, and a picture which I now know was an icon. The sun shone outside, and inside my mind there was an equal brightness.

My first words were defiant. I may still be wrapped in peaceful warmth, but that didn't mean I was ready yet for surrender to rules I found unacceptable.

"I am a lapsed Catholic," I began firmly. The priest nodded without surprise or even question. Of course I was. I told him about my day at Selly Park. It was a comprehensive account, leaving nothing out, but when I came to the moment in the chapel I found myself completely and hopelessly at a loss. Trying unsuccessfully to put it into words, I became incoherent and wept again. When I finished he was quiet for a few minutes. Then he asked what I wanted.

I replied instantly, without any doubt. "I want more of it".

He nodded again. I asked what I should do.

"Don't do anything," he said, "Just establish a – relationship – then when you're ready, but not before, only when you're ready, come to Mass or come and see me again".

He asked if I had read much. I said I hadn't, because although my sister had lent me some of her books I'd only glanced at them because they were too Americanised and emotional. "I'm a literary snob," I told him, "and they were rubbish".

Even as I spoke I knew that what I'd said was a lie. My only reason for not reading them was because they were religious.

The little priest smiled, amused again but gently so. He stood up and studied the bookshelves behind him. "I think I have just the one," he said.

He handed me "Did you receive the Spirit?" by Simon Tugwell.

He saw me off and I drove home, to read his book in the garden, sitting in a deck chair outside the dining room window in a clear, bright April afternoon. And before I'd reached the end of the second page I knew. I knew I was going to commit myself into the keeping of this new but ancient (and, it must be admitted, a very unfashionable) God. I knew that the book was opening a door through which I had been invited to step. I could still back out, but somehow I knew I wouldn't, for in a moment of revelation too deep and mysterious for me ever to put into a form of words, I had been touched by a personal God. I had felt the challenge of a sword on my shoulder, and for me challenges have always been difficult to resist. I had also felt the breath-taking touch of perfection. Perfection, an unbelievable sense of love, and a new and unutterable peace. How could I not accept this invitation? If the sounds I'd heard were not man-made, composed, rehearsed and conducted, then they must have been God-made, and any God who created such ineffable harmonies had my backing.

I knew enough psychology, though, to understand that experiences such as mine could – and certainly would - be explained away. I had been under stress, suffering from mental and physical fatigue. I'd been unhappy for some time without knowing why, and was therefore ripe for plucking. At a suitable moment some unexpectedly moving music, in an atmosphere tailor-made for such experiences, had swept me off into a mystical and emotional state where I would believe anything. Like an LSD trip, or a cult brainwashing, I was in the right place, in the right mood and in the right physical and emotional state for such phenomena.

True. But on the other hand, God chooses his moments with care, and I certainly wouldn't have listened to him at any other. And there comes a point when rationalisation is simply not enough. I did not *believe* there had been a personal encounter with God, I *knew* there had. And that knowledge would be enough take me into a totally new world, among new people and into a new awareness of myself and everything around me. But most of all, it was enough to carry me into an absolute and total awareness of the presence of God.

I must choose. Either to believe that the events of yesterday were the product of an overstressed psyche, or that they were true and unarguable. On 24th April 1978 I decided they were true, and by Chapter Two of Simon Tugwell's book I'd made the ultimate decision. My life was about to change.

Cases must rest solely on results. It isn't the experiences themselves that matter, only the effect they have.

"By their fruits you shall know them"

CHAPTER FIVE

Having made the decision to take to new waters, I dived in head first, not because I am naturally brave but because once something becomes unarguable there is really no point in arguing about it. And I simply couldn't deny the experience. As easy to say I had no sons, or that our colour television was really black and white.

The experience itself was going to need some careful and detailed analysis in order to be intelligibly accounted for to my social circle, but for now it was too bright and clear to need any explanation for myself. That would no doubt come later as I began to question, maybe, a fading memory. Meanwhile I was all set to accept the challenge and change course.

There would be difficulties, that was certain sure! In fact the path ahead looked as if it might be littered with sizeable boulders, and I quailed. For a start, how was I going to explain to all my non-Christian friends that I had committed that most antisocial of social crimes – Got Religion? Would they believe my story? I thought not. Would they strike me off their Christmas card list? I hoped not. In short, was I going to have any friends left at all? This was a question I wasn't even going to try to answer.

Then there was the even bigger problem of an agnostic husband and two sceptical sons, both of whom were steeped in rock music and socialist/anarchist philosophies.

"Oh well!" I said to myself, "We'll just have to cross these bridges one at a time". Then I spoke to God. "And as it's all your fault, you'll have to help me cross them".

Since that afternoon, I have tried many times to explain the charmed, graced life I led throughout the whole of the following summer. I think it was the childlike simplicity with which I not only embraced what the book told me, but believed it absolutely. Simon Tugwell said if one prayed one received answers, that miracles not only happened but were two a penny. Why should I doubt him, when I was so obviously the recipient of one?

That night I couldn't sleep. I lay flat on my back thinking about God, until the effort of trying not to disturb a slumbering spouse became too much and I slipped out of bed and crept down stairs. I knew what I was looking for but had no idea where to find it. The eight or so book cases scattered about the house were all crammed with volumes of all sizes and shapes in no sort of order, so finding one small book which I hadn't laid eye or finger on for years wasn't going to be easy. But I had all night for the search and I certainly wasn't going back to bed without it.

I found it in three minutes flat. It sat, small and squat, in the very first bookcase I investigated – a little black Bible with tiny print and leaves like tissue paper edged with gold. Inside the flyleaf, in familiar rounded handwriting with all the m's and n's looking like w's and u's, were the words "To Mary with fondest love from Mummie". I passed over that quickly. My mother had died twenty years before and I wasn't yet ready to accept, without a great deal of discomfort, the idea that she might have been right and myself wrong. Adolescent rebellion still lived on in my forty-odd-year-old bosom.

But I was more than ready to chance the little Bible. When I did the page fell open at Psalm 92. Not that this impinged on my consciousness in any way. Psalms, prophets, books and testaments had all merged long ago. But as I read that particular psalm, my heart almost leaped out of my dressing gown. I was entranced.

"*It is good to give thanks to the Lord,*" it said, "*and to sing praises to your name, O most High: To declare your loving-kindness in the morning, and your faithfulness every night. On an instrument of ten strings, on the lute and on the harp, with harmonious sound. For you, Lord, have made me glad through your work: I will triumph in the works of your hands*".

Since all this was undoubtedly the case, I read further and went very quickly to the New Testament, to the Gospel of St Matthew, reading with disbelief his account of the dynamic man who strode through the pages turning traditional views on their heads, making friends with all the low life and upsetting the hierarchy. I loved it. And I loved the man he was describing. But most of all I loved the freshness, the vigour and the absolute reality of it all.

There was no doubt in my mind that what I read was true. I stayed by the gas fire in our sitting room, engrossed in this most authentic of tales, until a less palatable truth came to me. Dawn was not very far off, and in not many hours' time I must get up and go to work. So I went back to bed but took my mother's Bible with me.

It stayed by my bedside, that little book, and I read it every night instead of crime and science fiction stories until, a few days later, it was replaced by a shiny new Good News Bible three times the size and weight and with rather less "Verily verilys" in. And over the next few days I finished Simon Tugwell's "Did you receive the Spirit?" and began putting it to the test.

The results were startling.

My first attempt at practical praying was entirely due to our elder son, Gerard, who was living in a bedsitter and had been corresponding with a girl he'd met in Bristol. She had gone Down Under for a year of adventure and challenge, but was apparently finding the challenge of Australia rather less appealing than the challenge of the Gerard revealed in his letters. So back she had come, home earlier than planned, and a great deal hung in the balance. I therefore flexed my budding muscles and said to my new/old Deity (who was nothing at all like the one I'd learned about at school, or at home for that matter) "If this is a good thing please make it good right away, so there's no doubt". And it must have been for he did. They've been together ever since.

Not that I have ever told either of them what I did. Suggesting to a young non-believer that he owes at least some part of his success with a girl friend to God rather than to his own charms would be, I felt, hardly tactful. Even worse when it was his own mother who had petitioned God in the first place. Besides, it was only true in the sense that had it not been a Good Idea, God would presumably have made it clear to both of them from the start. But as the weeks went by and the relationship prospered I grew more and more shy of admitting what I'd done. Perhaps after twenty or more years, God might be permitted just a bit of the credit.

But all this was to come. Today was only Day Two, and I was driving home wondering whether to continue straight there or make a detour to the supermarket. So I took a deep breath. "Please God," I said, "tell me which to do." and a few minutes later arrived at the place where decisions must be made. Left to the supermarket, straight on for home.

I laughed. Across the road to the left stood a sign proclaiming "Diversion". So I went home, and as I opened the front door the telephone rang. It was my husband to say he would be home early.

Yes, I know perfectly well that the sign would have been there, and my decision made for me, even without asking God for help. But I thought it was funny at the time, and I still do.

Cheered and emboldened, I flexed my new muscles a few times more and then decided to begin the daunting job of "telling my friends". The first attempt was disheartening. Sheila was an unmarried girl in her mid-thirties, bored with her job and with life in general and afraid she was never going to meet the man of her dreams. We lunched together on the Tuesday and I began my tale, but as soon as I reached the guitars she stopped me. "I'm sorry" she said, "I can't stand that sort of thing", so the conversation instantly became banal and stilted as we tried to think of less controversial topics. But I wasn't so easily put off, and on the following evening I visited my friend Marjorie in her top floor Bristol apartment. There I told my story from start to finish and waited for a response. She regarded me in silence.

"Are we still friends?" I asked, pulling a face.

She smiled faintly and nodded. "I think I'm jealous," she said.

"Oh you mustn't be," I cried, eagerly jumping in with what I already knew without question – that there was nothing special about *me*. "This is meant for *everybody,* you can have exactly the same if you want it". Then I suggested rather tentatively that since prayers seem to get answered, we should ask for something for her.

"What would you like?" I asked. This question was going to be repeated many, many times over the next few months.

Marjorie knew at once what she wanted. She had just finished a very painful affaire with a man called Andy, who still had some of her property. "I'd like to know where he is," she said, "without him knowing I know. And I'd like my things back".

"Okay," I said cheerfully and departed for my car. On the drive home in the dark, I told God that I knew he'd heard Marjorie and please could she have what she had asked for.

Next day, after work, I was cooking supper and waiting for my husband to arrive home when Andy rang from London. I must say at once that he had never done this before and never did it again, but that evening he was reminding me of a book I'd once borrowed from him. Please could I send it back.

So I asked for his address and he gave it..

Bemused but gleeful, I immediately phoned Marjorie and said "How's this for speed?" She replied that I didn't know the half of it. On arrival from work she had found all her things in the locker by her front door.

We were both stunned. "He doesn't waste much time, does he?" I laughed.

After that there was no holding me. I phoned or invited out all my non-believing friends one after the other, telling the story to each one and always finishing with the same question – "What would you like?" and, sometimes within two or three days or even less, the friends received their requests.

Kate was a long-standing friend from our newly-married, pram-pushing days in Nottingham. We hadn't met for some time, but I phoned her now and dived straight into my story for fear of losing my nerve. Her daughter had been suffering for years from anorexia. In answer to my question she said shyly that she'd like Vicky to be well. "Okay," I said. Two weeks later I rang her again.

"You've been on my conscience," Kate said, "I should have rung you. Three days after your phone call we had a card from Vicky to say she'd had her first period for two years". One of the symptoms of anorexia is that the girl stops menstruating. Kate, however, didn’t seem as happy as I expected her to be. The impression given was that while she was delighted with the result she wasn't quite as delighted with the manner of its getting! She would, I thought, have been very happy to find a nice, down-to-earth, reasonable explanation.

She had her chance a few months later. One Saturday morning I opened a harassed letter from her, saying her niece was threatening to come and stay. As she had done this once before with disastrous consequences, this was very definitely not a Good Idea, but Kate couldn't think how to avoid it. So she had written saying "A quick, urgent prayer please," and I sleepily obliged, sitting up in bed and sending up a brief call for action.

Two weeks later I rang for news. "Oh, it's okay," she said, "It all worked itself out neatly. I needn't have bothered you".

I was amused. Exactly what, I asked, had neatly worked itself out?

"Oh, Joe contacted his brother and they sorted out the problem between them".

Fine! Except that husband Joe had not been on speaking terms with his brother for years. But I didn't say anything, since Kate was not in the mood for giving God any credit, and we changed the subject. It was never taken up again. We met less and less frequently and somehow had less and less to say of any consequence when we did. When two people approach basic problems from opposing philosophies (Is this life all there is, or is there another after death?) intimate conversations, as opposed to merely social ones, quickly become sticky and usually end with frustrating abruptness when one finds oneself walking slap bang into the plate glass of the other's belief.

Over the next few months so many astonishing things happened that simply to put them in a list would be eye-crossingly boring. Yet to leave out that amazing period would not only be unfair, it would miss out the greatest fun I've ever had!.

There was Pat, for example, whose pigeons eventually came home to roost. She and I had spent the occasional happy hour in pubs, contentedly crying into our cider over the deficiencies of men in general and in particular the intransigence of our own. So when we met as usual, in a crowded lunchtime bar, she was certainly not expecting to talk about God. Her attitude was one of surprised but mild tolerance. If I wished to get myself hooked into "religion" that was my affair, but she herself was more interested in the problem of a difficult boyfriend – from whom she had no intention of parting! So when I asked her what she wanted, her request was a small, practical one. Her elderly mother had been offered a council flat and didn't know whether to accept it or not.

I decided to ask for a clear indication one way or another, with no possible doubt and as soon as could be managed. Next day I was told the Housing Department had issued an ultimatum. It was this flat or nothing and Pat's mother would lose her place on the list. Needless to say she took it. But Pat herself forgot the incident until I reminded her later. Meanwhile, the relationship with her gentleman friend was running into trouble and finally ended altogether. At this point Pat rang me. "You know the story you told me a few months ago?" she said, "Well, could you tell me it again please?"

I did. With astonishing speed she changed her philosophy, attended the seminars and became a leader of a local prayer group. She is still there.

Then there was Sheila, who had taken fright at the first mention of guitars, but who returned a month later to apologise.

"Sorry I stopped you in mid-flow," she said, "but I've always been frightened of emotionalism in religion and I thought you were going to go all Pentecostal on me. You can tell me the rest now, though, if you like".

Since 'the rest' consisted almost entirely of a subjective and emotional response to a sensory experience, I was in danger of sailing rather close to her 'Pentecostal' image and wasn't quite sure how to go about it. But she listened quite happily and, at the end, asked for a change in her life. A new job? A man? She didn't know exactly. Just something to send her in a new direction.

Next time I saw her she had met this wonderful man. She married him.

Practical praying had practical results in more ways than one – notably with my finances! Within three weeks of the Big Day the parish where my little priest held office was to have its Spring Fair. Although I lived outside its catchment area I had happily hitched my wagon to its star, and therefore felt called upon to donate something to the prize draw. My sherry intake had been growing higher and higher with the years – so much so that my elder son had once accused me of being one of the middle-aged, middle-class supermarket sherry-drinkers. My donation, then, had to be a bottle of Harvey's best. It was, after all, the least I could do. Harvey's best, however was at the time costing £2 a bottle (a considerable sum in those days when my entire housekeeping money for the week was only £20). Cash for the week was given to me on Friday mornings, so that particular week's allowance was going to be a little short and I would have to go carefully on my shopping trip.

I was sitting up in bed, drinking tea and doing sums in my head, when Geoffrey came in with an opened letter in his hand. He was laughing.

"Guess what!" he said, "We've had a cheque for £4 from the Vehicle and General receivers, so that's £2 for you and £2 for me".

Some time before, we had been the victims of an insurance company crash and had lost our premium. Now Geoffrey was handing me two crisp pound notes and the sherry was as good as mine.

Exceedingly amused by this evidence of God's care and attention (not to mention his speed and efficiency) in the beleaguered matter of my finances, I thought I'd give it another go when the phone bill arrived. The telephone bill in those days was my responsibility, since Geoffrey was adamant that he didn't want a phone and therefore refused to pay for one. The bill came to £85.72p. All I had in my bank account was £23. There was no question of earning more immediately, as I had only just left the insurance broker's office and was busy setting up a Monday-to-Friday paying guest service for the nearby Civil Service training centre and hadn't quite started yet. This was going to give me a great deal more personal freedom but less financial security because I wouldn't know from week to week how many guests to expect, if any, or how long they would stay. So I handed the bill over to God.

"It's your fault it's this big," I told him, "All those long-distance calls and the hours I've spent answering questions, the least you can do is help me with it".

In the same post there was a communication from a mail order company. "Introduce a friend and we'll pay you £5," it said. So I rang my new friend Cathy and asked if I could send in her name. She said yes, and I duly wrote £5 on a piece of paper.

During the course of that week someone commissioned a portrait for which I would receive £15, my sister Norah rang to say she'd won a premium bond and wanted to share it with me to the tune of £20. By the time a host of other small amounts had dribbled in, the total on my piece of paper, plus the £23 already in my account, came to £85.72p.

You have to laugh, don't you.

Then there was the £5 note I couldn't give away. Each time I tried, the note would turn up again, and when I handed over a fiver to my son John, felt in the pocket of my coat and found another nestling there, he stared at me in shock. "I wish I had that trick" he said.

I grinned back. "You could if you wanted," I told him, "if you believed what I believe".

All I can say about those months is that everybody smiled at me, colours were brighter, music was more beautiful, life was fun and absolutely everything I prayed for came about. Little Fr.Jim came to rely on me. When he lost his watch he asked me to find it for him, then spoilt his dignified entrance into church next morning by nodding at me and pointing to his wrist. My friend Joan rang one night in distress to say she'd lost something vital (I've forgotten what it was) and rang ten minutes later to say "Mary, you are handy! I went straight to it".

My husband, though, seemed less than amused by this 'trick'. After immediately finding his wallet after hours of fruitless searching, followed by a phone call to me, he said rather crossly "Don't go giving God the credit for that. I suddenly remembered where it was".

True. But who had prodded his memory?

The prayer answers just then came tumbling too fast to record or remember, but some of them revealed what I had suspected for some time. God has a marked sense of humour and his timing is perfect. Alex needed her psoriasis to be cleared up "for a special reason", and so it was. But it didn't stay cleared. In fact it returned with redoubled force, and shortly afterwards I learned why. Her "very special reason" had not been very laudable! Once again I was amused.

"Small things," people said, "Coincidences", "synchronicity" and "They would have happened anyway". But if two thousand coincidences follow two thousand prayers for them, and if when the prayers stop the coincidences stop too - that has to be too much of a coincidence! Synchronicity carried beyond expectation or logic and even beyond statistical possibility.

"But why do these things happen to you and not to us?" people asked, to which I replied "Because I believe they will and you obviously don't".

For me, after the first day, no further proof had ever been needed. Had I not been told "Ask and you shall receive?"

CHAPTER SIX

The fundamental change that came over me in 1978 seemed to me like a train going over the points. One minute I was heading in one direction and the next I was heading off somewhere new. Yet, at the vital moment and for a short while afterwards the only obvious change was in my own attitude. It was only as the train gathered momentum and the tracks led further and further away from their starting point that the terrain revealed itself as markedly different. My whole lifestyle, in fact, was being affected.

Mind, the train in this case picked up a remarkable turn of speed. This was as well, for my lifestyle was overdue for changing. Socially I did very nicely. There were plenty of friends happy to join me in drowning our assorted sorrows in wine and song – especially the song! Operatic societies are natural grow-bags for people wishing to escape reality, and the society I belonged to was no exception. Rehearsals, concerts and the Gilbert and Sullivan opera which devoured most of my leisure time every Spring, all these filled up my calendar very nicely. Yet it was never enough. I always seemed to need more dates outlined, more exciting things to look forward to after which life might become dreary again, so I would need more dates ringed.

Looking back, I see that in fact I had, to quote from Gilbert & Sullivan's Princess Ida, "Nothing whatever to grumble at". My life was lived in comfort and pleasant surroundings, I had an intelligent, kindly husband and two clever, charming and well behaved sons, and I drove the family car without let or hindrance – for the simple reason that Geoffrey couldn't and wouldn't drive it himself. I was a remarkably lucky woman, and the greater part of me knew it!

So what was wrong? I had no idea. I only knew that something indefinable was very definitely amiss.

Without a sense of purpose one can feel poor in the middle of plenty, depressed for no cause at all, so psychologists (amateur and professional) will have a great time concluding that because my life needed alteration, I subconsciously grasped the first real opportunity for change that presented itself. And this may easily be true. But there are limits, after all, to the effects of such chancy escapism, and I had grasped at passing opportunities before without any marked effect. I might easily have Got Religion for a while and then Got Something Else as soon as the religion grew harder and lost its charm. Anyway, the proof of a pudding is in the eating, and what I Got was not Religion but God. Or rather, God Got Me.

There is a big, big difference between Religion and God and at first I was filled with an almost desperate desire to explain this. Religion, I pointed out to the sceptics, can be anything one gives one's life and heart to. Money, art, career, sex, drugs, the pursuit of happiness. It is also the ritual, the ceremony, the trappings (which include all the man-made regulations) of an established Church.

This I was very anxious to disown. It seemed to me that all the terms one uses for God should be scrubbed out and new, fresh ones written in the place of the old - one which would better express what I knew and felt.

It wasn't the meaning of the words I wanted to change. The meaning was clear, true and brilliant and, it seemed to me, so gloriously self-evident that the whole world would be able to see for itself if only it looked in the right place. But the old words were so misleading, the over-used jargon so dismissed by society as irrelevant, that I was constantly looking for new ways of expressing old truths.

"It's not fair," I complained. "The old words are right, but if I use them no-one will listen. People sort of cringe and look away, as if God is an exploded myth in bad taste and somehow embarrassing".

As it was, I just became more and more frustrated. Even with priests like Fr Jim I was having difficulty describing my feelings in a way that matched his vocabulary and expectations. Nothing so sudden and life-changing, he seemed to feel, could last. Certainly nothing so unorthodox - and unorthodox is what I very soon became.

Not at once, though. At first I was only anxious to dive back into the Church I'd left, accepting it without too much criticism if not entirely without question. But this state of affairs didn't last long - just long enough to take me through the first vital few months, by which time I had enough confidence in my God, (as opposed to the old Establishment God whom I scarcely recognised) to start sifting the information I was being given.

Fr Jim had lent me his book and told me to go away until I felt like coming back, or until I had "established a relationship". This suited me perfectly, as the relationship seemed to have been born whole, as it were, hair, teeth and organs all in place and functioning strongly from its very first cry.

By the end of the first week I understood that the Person I was relating to was not only God but Jesus - and here again I was up against old and by now discredited jargon. To believe in - worse, to talk about - Jesus Christ was to have joined the 'Jesus freaks' of the '70s, the Bible-bashers, the 'Hallelujah brigade', none of whom were acceptable except to other freaks and bashers. So although I knew perfectly well who I wanted to speak about, I actually referred to him obliquely even to Fr Jim. To use the name Jesus, instead of Christ (the normal Church soubriquet) or The Universe (society's cover-all) branded me at once as having really and truly Got Religion. So I simply said "God" and left it at that. God, after all, is believed in, in one form or another, by all the world religions, however their view of Him may differ. And if asked, many non-believers admit rather grudgingly that yes, there is some power somewhere, though they wouldn't like to say exactly what or who or where it is. It was in order, therefore, to talk about God provided I didn't start preaching uncomfortable doctrines like the Ten Commandments - or refer to God's son by his now taboo name!

The following Sunday morning, when I was exactly one week old, I took myself to Fr Jim's church to Mass, and was amazed. From the first words of the very first hymn, everything was startlingly clear and meaningful. Truths leaped from every page, shouting at me so loudly that I looked around at the rest of the congregation, astonished at their calm, almost stolid composure.,

Didn't they realise what they were saying and hearing? How could they listen to such powerful words and remain unmoved? Why were they not on the point of tears, as I was, at the awe-inspiring truth and beauty surrounding us?

One hymn in particular attracted me. Both in words and melody "Lord Jesus Christ" held me in enchanted silence, unable to sing. Although I didn't know it at the time, it was to become of real significance over the years, popping up unexpectedly at moments of stress or anxiety as if to reassure me that I was after all on the right track. Even now, after all this time, finding it on the hymns list or hearing it unexpectedly sends an immediate shaft of warmth and reassurance, usually accompanied by tears, as if God is sending encouragement and hope right into the heart of my perplexity.

At the point of Communion, though, I suddenly knew I couldn't go forward with the rest to receive it. Not because God himself hadn't forgiven me or had told me not to come, but because I had some sorting out to do. I felt dishevelled and grubby and receiving such a magnificent gift for the first time in years would have felt like going to a party with uncombed hair, yellow teeth and dirty jeans. So I spoke to Fr Jim on the way out and asked to see him again.

"Of course," he said, "Give me a ring and we'll fix it", but meanwhile there was an ecumenical service to be held the following

Thursday at the local Anglican church and would I care to go to it? Would I? At that moment I would have gone to anything anywhere!

There was, however, a complication. I was about to burst forth upon a startled public once again, this time in the role of Saccharissa in 'Princess Ida', and the show was only a few weeks away. To my great annoyance and frustration, rehearsals were being held twice a week in readiness for a production in early June, and my time and energy were being diverted into theatricals when I wanted them for my marvellous new discoveries. From being a pleasant and exciting way of spending time, this singing business had suddenly become a nuisance. Even the prospect of a starring role, however small, wasn't enough. But it was too late to back out now. Rehearsals had gone too far and I had already let my fellow artistes down once. A second time was out of the question.

So it was with a rather delightful feeling of playing truant that I went with Amelia to Fr Jim's ecumenical service that Thursday. She'd been pleased to be invited, though still not asking questions - a monumental piece of tact on her part for which I was grateful, since I wasn't ready yet to admit things to Christians. Telling non-believers was exciting. Telling believers who had obviously been praying for me and (horror upon horrors!) watching me for signs of conversion, was quite another. That involved Pride and, for me at least, some loss of face. I hadn't confessed my change of heart to Amelia. Neither had I told my sister, which was of course unfair since it was entirely due to her persistence that I'd gone to Birmingham at all. However, fair or unfair, I was extremely reluctant to climb down.

In the Anglican church hall we all stood in a circle and prayed and sang, and the hymn we sang first of all was "Lord Jesus Christ". I was amazed. Gratitude to God for sending it again so soon had me fumbling in my bag for tissues to mop up the tears dripping down my chin.

Next day I went to see Fr Jim again.

Again he asked "What do you want?", and again I said "I want more of it. I want everything. Communion - the lot. But first I suppose I have to go to confession".

He looked at me in a considering sort of way. "Wait a bit," he said at last. "Don't be in so much of a hurry. I want to be a little more sure of you first".

I smiled but said nothing, knowing perfectly well he was worrying for nothing. He told me to come back again next week and we would discuss the matter of confession and the sacraments, but first he needed to know more about me, about my life until then, my way of thinking.

I had plenty of questions. Why did God demand that we praise Him all the time? Wasn't it rather conceited of Him? Why did Catholics maintain Jesus was an only child while other denominations maintained equally forcibly that he wasn't? I once even telephoned, rather late in the evening, to ask what one did with anger and resentment. "Give them to God," he replied.

But although Fr Jim was often amused and always understanding and helpful, his answers did not entirely satisfy me. In the end I decided to find out for myself. I spent many hours turning these thoughts over in my brain and reading all the books I could lay my hands on.

Meanwhile I was having a little trouble at home with a husband who was noticing, but pretending to ignore, the new Bible and the new Me. I was getting up early every morning to go to Mass and extraordinary things were happening. But above all I was paying an altogether different kind of attention to the man I had married. I was seeing him with fresh eyes, as though someone had just pulled back a rather dusty blackout curtain and revealed the person he had become. I was also feeling desperately sorry for what I felt sure was awful neglect over the years. But although he may have sensed what was going on in my head, I was afraid he wasn't too pleased about it. Like Kate, he may have liked what he was getting without liking the way it was coming about!

The new Me plus God was possibly less acceptable than the old Me without Him.

A few days later I telephoned my sister, who was tactfully restrained in her delight and contented herself merely with sending me some books in the post. And these books I actually read! I may have rather unfairly called myself a literary snob, but even the smallest crumbs of information were being scooped up wherever I found them. 'Nine o'clock in the Morning' and 'The Healing Light' shared my bedside table with the Bible and I ate them up like a starving puppy.

On Whit Sunday I went to confession. Not as simple as it sounds.

Complications began the night before. I had made an appointment with Fr Jim for four o'clock next day, uneasily aware that we'd invited friends for dinner that evening and I would be hard pressed to be ready for them. But confident, as usual, that anything can be achieved if one puts one's mind to it, I calculated that a quick half hour away from home in the afternoon could easily be made up by some forethought and a bit of organisation.

There were, however, other problems. I hadn't been to confession for so many years that I'd forgotten how to do it. Memory conjured up past ordeals in a small and rather frightening black cabinet which smelt of dusty wood and kneelers, and of peering through a rectangle of trellis at a dark silhouette. There had always been the sound of breathing, with a disembodied voice asking me how long it was since my last confession. This of course I had invariably forgotten, so I invented a date just to be obliging. I could never remember my sins either, and simply went through the sort of list that sounded right but which had very little to do with the facts. So I was nervous about this appointment, even though Fr Jim had reassured me that the system nowadays was not in the least like how I remembered it all.

I was also caught up in a personal perplexity and lay in bed next to a husband who could have done nothing to help me even if he hadn't been snoring. So in a sort of despairing frustration I cried out to the God who, I was assured, would come to my assistance, and mentally shook my fist at him.

"Okay," I told him firmly, "If you're really there, prove it”.

In Norah's books I'd been reading about something called the gift of tongues. Apparently this was a gift from the Holy Spirit that we could use or not, as we chose. It seemed we had control over it, but that if we began speaking God would do the rest. So in a spirit of research I put this new information to the test and opened my mouth.

What came out was astonishing. Yet somehow I wasn't astonished. The words were strange, the language foreign and incomprehensible, the sentences came and went with commas and full stops, and finally condensed themselves into a small hook which went round and round in a recognisable pattern.

Finally I asked what they meant, and the words came clearly into my head. "I love you, nothing matters. I love you, nothing matters", at which point I promptly went to sleep.

Next morning I awoke to a rainy day and the prospect of guests for dinner. Geoffrey and I went shopping in the car. Outside the supermarket it broke down. I was obliged to drive home without using reverse gear and with the horrid realisation that I would now have to walk a mile and a half each way to church in the rain when there was an important meal to cook and a table to lay. Which in turn presented me with yet another problem.

For nearly three weeks I had put off telling my husband what had happened to me in Birmingham. He was not going to be pleased.

I waited until almost the last moment, then said "I'm going to church".

"You're going where?" Obviously, but understandably in the circumstances, he thought he had misheard.

"To church" I replied, "to confession".

Nervousness by this time was probably making me sound aggressive, which didn't help.

"Ah!" he said, and carried on polishing a wine glass. "I think you'd better explain".

So I did. As expected, he was not happy with the explanation. "My dear," he said with heavy patience, "you are being conned. But of course you will do as you think fit, as long as you never try to convert me".

I promised I never would, put on my raincoat and headscarf and began my mile and half walk in the rain.

Having arrived at Fr Jim's super-modern church with its space-age roof and pine pews, I stood inside the entrance dripping wetly onto the parquet floor, wondering where to go. By nature I am fine with grand designs, but inevitably stumble over the details of life, and realised that the confessional was not going to declare itself with neon lights, and that I would have to search for it. A woman clack-clacked through the church in court shoes and would have passed me with a polite nod, but I stopped her. When in doubt, ask, has always been my maxim!

"Excuse me," I said, "I'm looking for the confessional".

The woman in the court shoes didn't seem at all surprised, but simply pointed to a pine door on the other side of the church above which a little light shone modestly. "You'll see the door is ajar," she told me, "Just push it and walk in".

I did. Fr Jim was sitting in a small but comfortable room, not at all intimidating and in fact rather cosy. Facing him was another chair, into which I was invited to place myself, with coat, bag and scarf steaming gently in the warm air.

I explained how because the car had broken down I'd been obliged to walk, and hoped such resolution would convince him of my serious intent. I didn't add that I had also run the gauntlet of a not-terribly-pleased husband engaged in dinner preparations, as that would have entailed going into more detail than I had the energy for.

He opened the proceedings by reading a short passage from the Bible about taking out my heart of stone and giving me a heart of flesh, adding that although I might think it wasn't altogether appropriate in my case it was a good place to start all the same. Then for the rest of the time we simply talked. It was all very normal, and the relaxed atmosphere and comfortable chairs were so far from my memory of the past that by the time I'd talked myself out it was seeming all too easy. Perhaps I hadn't suffered enough. Early conditioning rose up to warn me that because it had all been rather delightful this confession wouldn't qualify!

Then Fr Jim raised his hand over me and quite clearly and distinctly said words of absolution. And forgiveness came sweeping over me with such force that I almost fell out of my chair. Power was tangible and Love a reality. Fr Jim told me to say one 'Our Father' before I left, and then I rather hesitantly told him about speaking in tongues the night before.

"I understand it gives you a peaceful sort of feeling," he said. He looked quite wistful. I replaced my still dripping coat and scarf and went to one of the front pews to say my Our Father. Then I walked home.

Actually I didn't walk, I floated. The rain was warm and fresh and invigorating. Everyone I passed smiled at me. I was wrapped in a joy even deeper and greater than had enveloped me in Norah's spare bedroom three weeks before, a joy so sparkling, yet so peaceful, that it was like standing on tired feet in a mountain stream, or feeling one's hair lifted in a July breeze straight from the sea, or lying in a soft bed, warm and relaxed and ready for sleep. Except that sleep was far from my thoughts. Happiness had raised my energy levels and the walk home was accomplished with astonishing speed.

Dinner was ready on time and delicious, despite my defection, but although our guests had my polite concern they only had a small veneer of attention. Conversation was lost in a lovely hazy mist so that next morning I couldn't remember any of it. I only hoped the dinner talk hadn't been so inane that everyone else had forgotten it too, but relied on my intelligent and witty husband to make up for my own deficiencies.

Next day was Pentecost Day, Whit Sunday when the Holy Spirit descended on the apostles where they cowered in an upper room and turned them from frightened men into confident believers. With the car still out of action I once more walked to church, this time to Mass and this time to go with the rest of the congregation to the altar - to receive in my hands the small white round of bread which had suddenly become so important. Then I joined the others in the church hall for coffee and biscuits and smiled beatifically on surprised (but, I hoped, pleased) parishioners. I told one or two of them that it was my Big Day and they congratulated me. Then I changed my shoes and floated home again.

It was still raining but I really didn't care.

CHAPTER SEVEN

I met Cathy in unlikely circumstances and she endeared herself to me straight away. Because I felt trapped by Princess Ida when I wanted to be out looking for prayer groups, I dropped in on the first one I stumbled over. Amelia had already been there, and had made me jealous by going without me, so although she said it was not the sort I was looking for I went anyway.

It was a very quiet group, very meditative, no singing, in fact nothing very much at all - only seven people sitting in a small room in absolute silence and candlelight. One of the seven had read a short Bible passage and switched off the electric light, so it should have been peaceful. Perhaps it was for everyone else. But I wasn't ready yet for enforced inactivity, being still only a baby, and the breathings and shiftings and occasional tummy rumblings only filled me with the urge to giggle. When the candle was blown out and proper light switched on again, I turned to my neighbour and saw she was a pleasing person with shoulder length brown hair and an undeniable gleam in her eye. We eyed each other and a *je ne sais quoi* passed between us.

"The plumbing was a bit noisy tonight," she said. That was enough for me. We were going to be friends.

We met again a few weeks later, when Princess Ida was over and out of the way. All I wanted was to be joined with fellow Christians in any activity - any at all, so I hurled myself into Fr Jim's parish drama club which was rehearsing for a play called 'Friends and Neighbours'. I was to play the part of a Russian woman scientist with a heavy accent, get nicely drunk on vodka and chase a good looking young man named Mike around a stage sofa. Cathy was in charge of props, which of course included the sofa.

Things were, however, moving on in other directions at some speed. After spending my summer in a state of constant astonishment, after amazing happenings both little and large, of prayers being answered and friends being apprised of the cause, my new security was suddenly taken from me. The rug, it seemed, was being pulled from under my feet. Fr Jim was to be transferred and in August he left the parish.

Here was my first challenge. The first real testing of my beliefs. I supposed it was time I took a few steps on my own without the support of a Holy Priest of the Church who, though seeming sometimes a bit nonplussed by my enthusiasm (and by the trail of small miracles which apparently littered my bouncy spiritual path), had nevertheless been a wonderful bulwark during the past months. I had in fact become rather dependent, even if he did treat me with a certain amount of caution. There was that in his attitude which suggested he might be thinking "Light the blue touch paper and retire".

One day I beamed at him and said "I think you think I'm going to burn myself out".

"Yes" he replied.

I gave a Cheshire cat grin and said "We'll see".

Now I was going to have to do without him, so I prayed for someone suitable to take his place. Three weeks after he'd left, a new young curate arrived - not in Fr Jim's parish but in my own, the one I should have been going to all along. It was his match that lit the blue touch paper.

To rewind a little, Amelia and I had been hunting all this time for a real, proper prayer group, along the lines of Selly Park, where we could find those elusive seminars. The kind of group which would accept without question my small miracles because they were two a penny for them too. There had to be one somewhere, and wherever it was I intended to find it.

We eventually ran one to earth at a convent in Clifton, where we were assured that Days of Renewal were actually held once a month. "Just like Birmingham," I told my sister happily. We arranged for her to stay with us for the weekend so she and Amelia and I could all attend together, and presented ourselves on the Big Day with large expectations and a packed picnic basket.

The day didn't disappoint us, although the hall and chapel were considerably smaller than Selly Park, which made everything more intimate. The place was filled to the doors. The singing in tongues during Mass was just as beautiful, although different in an unidentifiable way. At the end of it a tall, dark young man was introduced to us all as Fr Peter, and we were told he was about to 'take up his appointment' as curate at my own local church up the road - into which I had not yet so much as poked my nose. So I flung myself at him and announced that I had just asked God for him, and that I was one of his new parishioners.

He was surprised but obviously delighted and turned up on my doorstep only a few days later to bask with me in a happy glow of mutual esteem. He was as relieved to find a kindred soul in his new congregation as I was to find one in my own parish presbytery, and we exchanged views and hopes in gathering excitement. Within an hour or so we had set up our own prayer group - in my house - and I was to share the leadership.

So soon, so close!

By this time I was a bit breathless. Things were moving at a cracking pace. In the next parish there was apparently an embryo prayer group just about to embark on a first set of seminars. So - naturally - I plunged into that too.

Seminars entail seven weeks of study, meditation and talks. We were divided into groups, and at the end of the seven weeks my leader placed his hands on my head and prayed for the Holy Spirit to descend upon me.

There was no doubt I was descended upon, but the descent was unexpectedly painful. I was a merry infant no longer, happily toddling beside an all-beneficent God, holding his hand with casual confidence. I was suddenly asked to grow up a bit, and the process hurt. I felt as if a magnifying mirror had been held up in front of me and I saw, with awful clarity, the spots and blemishes I'd been hiding under my make-up. Feeling rather like a small onion being gently but firmly peeled, I was horrified at each new brand of vanity and insecurity that came to light with every layer. It was tempting to think this new pain was a horrible mistake of mine, or God's, or - worse - a dreadful kind of retribution. But it seemed to me merely that this was the first stage in what looked like being a long haul. Self revelation was coming as a shock, but I hoped that the sooner it was over the sooner I might get back to the first careless rapture.

It reminded me a little of marriage after the honeymoon. Something to be worked at, and through. And by Christmas I definitely had a new image of myself. Our infant prayer group was beginning to overfill my dining room and I was leader of a hopeful gang of new babies.

Promotion was coming fast. I was not at all sure I was ready for it. Looking back I freely admit I wasn't, but God's sense of timing is peculiar to himself and in my case over-confidence was rushing in where angels had trodden before me.

As it turned out, Fate (in this case the bishop) once again took a decisive if unwelcome hand. The elderly parish priest in my new parish had just retired and a new one arrived who didn't need a curate. Worse still, he firmly and unequivocally disapproved of prayer groups. So we were turned out like orphans in the storm with nowhere to do our praying, praising and singing, and after only six months Fr Peter went away again.

My second bulwark having been removed in under a year, I was beginning to think God might be trying to tell me something.

The events of the autumn had given me a great deal to think about. Not only was I going through a sort of forced growth, rather is if I'd been placed willy nilly in an over-warm greenhouse, I was now coming up against problems that were both unfamiliar and unexpected. I was discovering that Christians were just as human as anyone else and very often badly behaved. And I was coming to be regarded with suspicion from both sides at once - by cradle Catholics for having charismatic leanings, and by non-Catholics for being a Catholic. I was, in fact, finding out - not without pain - that in churchy matters, as in plenty of others, non-conformity just Doesn't Do! In so many ways that eradicating them was impossible, I was sticking out like a daffodil in a rose bed.

To start with, I was asking too many difficult questions. Why was the Anglican Eucharist unacceptable? Why were priests celibate when the first pope, St Peter himself, obviously had a wife (He had a mother-in-law, anyway!). And why did the Church treat women as second class Christians when Jesus himself had very clearly behaved as if they weren't? The answer I'd been given for that (by a priest) was that men were to women as Jesus was to his Church, but this explanation merely exasperated me. It suggested a divinity for men but only a basic humanity for women. I threw it out.

These questions were put to some very wise and learned people in authority (all men!), but it took some years for these irritating knots to be unravelled, mostly by me, to my own satisfaction, and only after a great deal of reading, reflection, thought and of course prayer.

There were, however, plenty of silver linings to the clouds that from time to time dripped rain upon my head. I was making some very good friends.

With Maryrose it was love at first sight. We met at a Leaders' meeting, and the friendship stuck fast with the superglue of shared pain, experiences and a whole lot of laughter. Her family became my own and I developed territorial rights over their guest bedroom.

I met Joan at a Myers Briggs workshop, where we all learnt our principle character traits in the form of a personality profile. It seemed that she and I shared the same basic characteristics, a fact we both appreciated - especially when one of us lapsed (typically, I have to admit) into sudden and terrifying bouts of stupidity. It was always nice to know someone else could be just as daft.

There were others, but those three, Cathy, Maryrose and Joan, became essential anchors of support and understanding when they were most needed. We all had the same kind of solid faith in everyday miracles which I had taken for granted from the start – but which surprisingly few Christians shared. Those who did share it mostly belonged to prayer groups, and our combined get-togethers were exciting events full of anecdotes and jubilation. Everyone prayed together, for each other and for everyone else, and the news of success encouraged us to pray even more. We sang and cried and laughed and then sang again, because we were all new together, babies in a world of Spirit which itself seemed only just to have been reborn into a seemingly stale established church. Of course our enthusiasm was extreme and possibly open to abuse. A wary observer might have suggested that some people who stood with raised arms and closed eyes did do because, in that place and at that time, it was The Thing To Do. But people who were shamming didn't sham for long. Either their pretence became a surprising reality, or they left! Besides, a great many of the sceptics admitted to cheering at concerts and football matches so where, I asked them, was the difference?

One little Irish lady with white hair and an entrancing brogue was so angry at our first seminar that she marched up to Fr Peter and shook her fist at him. "You're all a lot of Billy Grahams," she shouted. But three weeks later her own arms went up in the air. She was astounded.

So was I astounded. Constantly. Everywhere I looked and everywhere I went extraordinary things were happening, some of them so unobtrusive that it was only afterwards that I recognised their significance. Some were just plain funny. Mark, the handsome hero in our play 'Friends and Neighbours' asked me one evening at rehearsal what went on in my house every Sunday night. I suggested he came and found out for himself, so he did. From then on we chased each other round the stage on Wednesday evenings and prayed together in my dining room after tea on Sundays.

Neither of us knew then that eventually he would become a group leader himself, like Pat, my pubbing friend whose mother was comfortably settled in her council flat. And like Cathy, who had had a life-changing experience of her own in the very same week as mine and who was a founder member of our embryo prayer group. When the new priest took over the parish and Fr Peter moved away, the combined Christ the King prayer group became home to everyone. Everyone, that is, except me. I went to help Fr Peter set up a new group in his new parish, and from then on began a sort of minor career in nursing seedling communities. It kept me on the move for years, and I was so busy nurturing new prayer groups up that I never seemed to belong to one myself.

I still don't.

CHAPTER EIGHT

I had a problem. In fact I had rather a lot, but this was to do with my correspondence, which at the time was fairly extensive. Emails were unknown to ordinary people like me in 1978, and I was trying to express my new *joi de vivre* to friends and family and couldn't find any appropriate cards to do it with. I felt they would neither understand nor appreciate the cards one finds in religious bookshops, with a Biblical reference for every quote or picture. I wasn't at all sure I appreciated those myself, coming as I did straight from the world of Monty Python and Hi de Hi. And if I jibbed at them, my friends and family certainly would. Not that there is anything wrong with overtly religious material, providing one believes in the relevance of the scriptures being quoted. I could hear some of my acquaintances reading a Bible quotation and saying "So what?" To a non-believer, one might as well quote Tennyson as evidence for the existence of King Arthur.

To add to the problem, I was jibbing even more at many of the secular cards. These seemed to be getting coarser and more vulgar by the day, each one sicker and less funny than the one before. So when Christmas came round again for the second time since C-for-Conversion day, I drew two designs, had them printed in black on blue card at the local quick-print shop, bought some standard envelopes (which of course the cards had been cunningly designed to fit) and sent them off.

They were a spectacular success. So next year I drew twice as many and printed more than I needed. My sister and two friends bought the remainder and I was in business.

One day in the following Spring, Norah wondered if the matter could be put on a proper footing and how would I like to do the whole thing commercially? Then she offered me a thousand pounds.

I said I'd think about it, but the thinking took no time at all. I was working as a telephone salesperson at the time and hated the job more every time I picked up the phone. So how could I refuse such an offer?

I didn't, of course. The chance was a perfect plum. Not only could I satisfy the burning ambition to share all these wonderful discoveries with the whole world, I would be spending my time on what had merely been a delightful hobby. The fun was going to be legitimate! So within a few weeks Norah and I were sitting with bank managers and solicitors, and I was juggling with some very basic problems.

Where, for example, did one start? Should I design the cards first, or cut them to standard envelope size? And what about the plastic envelopes to stuff them in? On such questions do whole empires depend!

The plastic envelope problem solved itself with no trouble at all. Having decided on the most common - and therefore the cheapest - envelope sizes, I set out to look for the requisite plastic bags and rang some local packaging firms. Within minutes I had found a manufacturer who was at that very moment setting up seventy thousand packets in exactly the right sizes, and would I like him to run off another couple of thousand for me at reduced rates?

I laughed, jumped up and down and cried "Hallelujah" a few times, then went out to buy the envelopes. Then all that was necessary was to create the designs, have them printed, fold and stuff them into my mint-new packets and, finally, market them. A mere trifle!

But we had at least begun and Firefly Art and Design was born. We threw a small party to celebrate. And because the name was important we had to baptise that too.

Long hours, days even, had been spent searching books, Bibles, poetry and our collected subconscious for a name that would be right. Then, early one morning, I lay in bed reflecting on the fire of the Spirit and how small we would be, yet hopefully how effective. And the image of a tiny, flying thing that glowed in the dark appeared before my closed eyes. I rose abruptly from my couch and shouted "Firefly! Of course!" Then I dialled Norah's number in Birmingham and shouted the same thing down the phone to her. She didn't, of course, have the remotest idea of what I was talking about and it took me several minutes to go from inspired incoherence to a reasonable explanation. It was, after all, fairly early in the morning.

Looking back, I think Norah and I were brave because we were innocent. She contributed the money, since I didn't have any, but as she lived in Birmingham and I lived in Bristol she couldn't help much with practical details except on intermittent visits. Not that I minded. It was so delightfully satisfying to be designing my own letterheads and logos, setting ourselves up with telephone ledgers and petty cash books and Small Business advisors.

At precisely the same time that God was providing us with plastic packets, he was also finding us a printer. Bob had been on stage with me in "Princess Ida" and up to now had been making fudge in a small factory in the North of Bristol. The demand for fudge, however, was growing less and less and he wished to expand his business, so had bought himself some printing presses and set up in partnership with a well established, *bona fide* printing friend. He agreed to print my cards at a rate I could afford..

Apart from hoping he wouldn't get the two ventures mixed up and get fudge on my designs or, even messier, print my designs onto the fudge, I was happy with this. So we learned our trades together, which was just as well. There were too many times when the ignorance of one of us proved to be a cheering consolation for the other's red face, so neither could feel superior.

Firefly's market, we decided, should be the world of prayer groups, convents and parish shops, and this we intended to tap into via Her Majesty's Mail. So we got ourselves a freepost address, designed some order forms and set about creating our first catalogue. This was a simple affair (we certainly couldn't afford anything else) on folded A2 shiny paper, with all the cards and letterheads and notelets printed in red with descriptions of their true sizes and colours marked alongside.

It was immense fun, especially when I went to collect my very first batch of cards, all fresh and new and smelling of ink. After they had all been folded and packaged with their own printed slips inside, then everything was ready for our first mailshot. A small army of helpers came for a joint stuffing session, to sit at our old refectory table filling large brown envelopes with folded catalogues and turning the day into a party par excellence. We ate sandwiches and drank coffee and told stories and laughed, and in my album there's a photograph of Norah and me standing beside the result - two huge mail bags. Four months of planning, inspiration, frustration and grinding closework, plus a good few heartaches, had come to a triumphant conclusion.

We had done all we could. The rest was now up to God and our customers.

Our Firely flew for three years precisely. In the Autumn before its demise we held two exhibitions, one at a shop on the Gloucester Road run by a young Pentecostal friend, and the other in my own home. Both were dignified by formal invitations on specially designed cards, and at both, in our best frocks, we dispensed glasses of wine to our guests, took orders and sold a great deal of stationery.

The organisation of these shows and the hard physical labour involved in transporting tons of paper and card from home to car to shop and back again had been exhausting and time consuming - but the sheer fun of them, the excitement, the satisfaction of seeing a shop filled with displays of our own handiwork, and the sight of a large (but I hoped tasteful) sign over the shop door announcing "Firefly Art and Design" in big letters, was worth every aching muscle. Those days will live on in my memory until I stop having one.

But we couldn't beat the juggernauts, those mighty companies who produce their cards in hundreds of thousands, even millions, and could therefore price them lower than it cost us to produce one thousand. By then we had two salespersons who trotted happily from shop to shop, sometimes from door to door, and no matter how many times they came home with filled order books and bouncing enthusiasm, I finally realised that taking all the hidden costs into account, every card we sold was actually making a loss. This was a shock to me, but was even more difficult for my salespersons to accept. "People are buying them," they argued. This was true, but the hard fact was that the more people bought, the more loss I made.

Then the Inland Revenue took a hand. They kept telling us we were not only making a profit but were making one so vast that we could afford to pay them four thousand pounds in tax. It would have been funny if it hadn't been exasperating and worrying, and since we were struggling to cover our costs and hadn't in fact made any profit whatever yet, we finally bowed to market forces and closed ourselves down.

Not, though, before we'd created unique logos for firms scattered about the country, produced four notelets, several sets of letterheads, five message cards, four greetings cards, six post cards and twenty Christmas cards. I had composed hand-made individual greetings cards on commission, drawn with fibre tip pen onto white shiny card, and spent hour after hour drawing, preparing things for the printer, typing official letters, answering the telephone and visiting wholesale stationers. I had shopped for stamps and pens. When my drummer son wasn't around to do it for me in his spare time, I had folded cards and notelets, counted them and shoved them into packets. I had entered orders into order books, made out invoices, counted packets into jiffy bags and posted them off to waiting customers. I had learned to separate colours onto tracing papers, how to keep accounts, how to be in four places at once and how, no matter how carefully one designed an order form, someone invariably misunderstood it.

Best of all, I had travelled around the area, giving Firefly talks to communities and prayer groups and women's groups and old peoples' clubs. I had set up my stall at fairs and conferences and carried my wares in a portable, wooden stand specifically made for me by my son's carpenter friend, and told the story of my conversion and the birth of Firefly. I even took myself off to the North of England on a sales trip, in a spanky new hired car because my husband was afraid my own wouldn't have arrived at its destination. What's more, I had loved every minute of it.

Some of the cards had been overtly religious, but for the most part they weren't. Of course, as my baker remarked one day, "They may not be religious but they've all got double meanings". This was undoubtedly true, but then that was the whole idea.

Unfortunately, most religious bookshops and stationers require their messages to be positively, unequivocally Bible-based, so we were more popular in the secular market. This should have been disappointing but wasn't. Hadn't the secular world been my target all along?

A three-year venture into the knives-out, blood-letting world of commerce was an exciting and extremely useful lesson - what would now be described as a learning curve – and one that I enjoyed but have no wish to repeat. As it took some time for her investment to return home to her Bank account, I doubt if Norah wishes to either. But neither of us would willingly have missed the experience. Apart from the fact that we'd both enjoyed ourselves, who knows who was touched in the heart, or tickled in humour, towards a God they never knew existed?

CHAPTER NINE

In those days I was a very busy person, in the heart of the action. Whatever was going on, that is where you'd find me. So, at precisely the moment when our little Firefly fluttered off into happy retirement, I was learning for the first time about Billy Graham's Mission England. How it had all happened without me up to now was a mystery. The only explanation I could think of was that I'd been too engrossed in my own plans to have an eye or an ear for the rest of the world, but I had somehow missed all signs of the structure which had been in place for almost a year.

Billy Graham had promised a visit to Britain for 1984 and big advance plans were being made by all the churches. Naturally, when these plans finally swam into my already dizzy orbit, I plunged myself into the current. Mission England was a national project covering three years altogether - one (this one) to prepare, one for the week-long open air meetings, and the last to tidy up.

It was a hugely ambitious programme and it not only kept me busy, it opened my eyes to the true state of the Church - the Christian church, that is, not just the RC part of it - and underlined all the discoveries I had been making privately since 1978. For I was neither fish nor fowl, uneasy with any label and regarded with, at best, kindly caution and, at worst, downright suspicion by Catholics and non-Catholics, believers, non-believers, priest, vicar or minister.

Personally I suspect the real reason for all these separate denominations has always been less theological than psychological. People go where they're happiest, where their personalities feel most at home. The ebullient will sing and dance, praise and exult; the ritualists will be inspired by ceremonies and incense and long, rich robes; and the quiet, reserved worshipper will go for quiet, reserved prayers from prayer books and nice, safe, singable hymns. There are also the passive believers who only go to church twice a year, if at all, and are happy to allow Authority to get on with things as they see fit, and the activists who think religion means serving on committees. Finally, there are those who favour the egalitarian approach, considering it their duty to be up with the leaders and always having plenty to say - mostly negative - about whatever is going on.

Even before Mission England I was already coming to believe that all these attitudes were probably right in their own way, and that all organisations need a healthy mix of watchers, doers, ritualists and revolutionaries. Even God's. Especially God's! As for me, I had been introduced into a sphere where people not only believed in positive gifts of the Spirit but were prepared to use them, and I'd been filled from the start with a probably terrifying zeal for these extraordinary phenomena. I had even, apparently, been given some of them myself, if only temporarily, not least of which was an unshakeable faith in the power of prayer.

The trouble with having so many different brands of faith, though, is that each type of believer seems to feel his or her own way of praying and worshipping and behaving is the only way to pray, worship and behave. Worse still, some feel positively threatened by their counterparts. "This is the way to heaven," they say, "Do as we do and you'll be saved. Follow your own way and we'll call you a cult - or even the anti-Christ - and consign you to the gnashing of teeth in outer darkness.".

Fear is astonishingly infectious. It seems to feed on itself. This means that in time some denominations are tempted to teach their followers to avoid all contact with the rest, like Victorian mamas removing their skirts from contamination with traders' mud. And sometimes the Catholic Charismatic Renewal, that part of the Church I had tumbled into, which believed the gifts were to be used, and used them, was occasionally vilified even by its own clergy.

I once heard a passionately conservative Catholic priest (who had obviously never heard of the Second Vatican Council) tell his congregation in a homily that "there are some people trying to put the Holy Spirit in the place of Christ".

I was astonished. For a Man of God who presumably believed in the Trinity, this was not only a remarkable statement. It was beyond belief! And to someone like myself, coming back after a fairly long absence into a Church in the throes of change, such statements were agonising. I never knew whether to laugh or cry and often did both.

So to be involved so closely with the Billy Graham Road Show was an Experience. It certainly changed my thinking because it opened me up to new aspects of God and spirituality, new realisations and new doubts, as old truths were silhouetted against the delightful new background of mutual tolerance.

Busy as I was in two fronts, as the only RC on the Women's Task Group (where 25 or so ladies worked and prayed together to organise events) and as one of the only 20 RC counsellors out of a total of 2,000-odd, I was deeply impressed by the whole thing. The atmosphere in the huge, packed football stadium was awe-inspiring. Every night the numbers there grew until not only the stands but half the pitch was filled, and so many were going forward to commit themselves that by the end of the week there was a call out each night for all counsellors, whether officially on duty or not. We found ourselves dealing with sometimes ten new, hopeful, dewy-eyed disciples at a time - asking them if they knew and understood the commitment they were making and which church they had come from, or wished to go to.

After spending several hours typing with the follow-up team, being entertained by the guest singers and filled with tea and buns at intervals, it was a case of finding my car, in the dark, in a very large field where normal landmarks disappear and other peoples' cars look exactly like one's own. By the end of the week I was reduced to sticking a huge white card on my windscreen with the words "Yer 'tiz" on it in big black letters. Happily this did the trick, beckoning to me whitely through the gloom, and I was free then to drive home in the early morning, watching the sun rise, amazed and inspired by what was happening to the good people of Bristol.

Mission England was, to me, a perfect example of the Church Getting it Right for a change. Billy Graham was inviting RCs into his road show, and RCs were not only permitted to accept his invitation but in many cases were even being encouraged. And all the other churches were working together in what looked like happy unison. Was this the beginning of real Christian Unity?

Now, I believe it to have been a foretaste of what is to come - unity at the lowest level short-circuiting the conferences and commissions and councils at the top. For we have been told by all the contemporary seers (and I believe it) that unity, when it comes, will come directly from God. Like the Berlin Wall, hostility and bigotry will crumble suddenly away and be seen for what they were. Not God-ordained but man-made.

CHAPTER TEN

Of all the dramatis personae in this adventure, the one character who had never appeared so far was Mary, the mother of Jesus. Somehow she and I never seemed to get on. Perhaps she reminded me too much of the headmistresses of my convent boarding schools - all three of them - tall, austere, forbidding and naturally, being Holy Nuns, totally virginal. Not my cup of tea!

So it was a surprise when this lady made a positive move to enter my life. An even greater surprise was the personality that emerged when she did.

It all began early on Thursday morning. I was lying in bed, worrying. Well, panicking actually. John, our younger son, had been living for some months in an expensive flat in Clifton, sharing it with two other young men. These had been absent for weeks and consequently hadn't been around to pay their share of the bills, the most recent of these being a rate demand for £280. John couldn't pay it. I couldn't pay it. His father wasn't going to pay it. And there was a Court summons for next day which John would not be attending because he was due to play the drums for his band at a London gig.

What I felt he really needed was a bedsitter with a coin-in-the-slot meter and only the rent to pay, but Bristol was knee-deep in students chasing too few bedsitters. So John was trapped with his bill for £280 (a fair amount of money in the 1980s), and a Court summons which he would not be obeying.

I myself was extraordinarily busy, with too much to do in too little time, and a large chunk of this particular day was going to be taken up with the problems of a much loved but beleaguered friend who was coming to be cheered up. I didn't feel capable of cheering her up. I didn't feel capable of cheering anyone up. In fact I seemed to have come round again to the same state of desperate busyness I was in when the whole story began in 1978. So I lay in bed, stiff with anxiety, and prayed.

I have always been either blessed, or cursed, with a strong, visual imagination. Fine, when one pictures sunlit vistas and happy events, but a very different proposition when the images are of falling downstairs or loved ones in car crashes! Thus it was with no great surprise that I found myself, that morning, walking slowly up a typical cottage garden path. On either side were country flowers, roses, delphiniums, sunflowers, hollyhocks and sweet smelling herbs and shrubs. The cottage door was ajar and tempting, so I stepped through it, rather hesitantly, into a tiny vestibule with an open door to the left leading to a cosy parlour. To the right another wide open door led to a large kitchen. Its ceiling was low and hung with herbs. The window overlooking the path was deep and recessed, with a bowl of fresh flowers glowing in a pool of sunshine. Facing me was a long kitchen range, with an oven door standing open and a kettle steaming gently on the hob. Between myself and them was a long refectory table on which a number of small cakes sat fragrantly on their cooling trays.

To the left were wide French windows with curtains blowing gently in a soft breeze, and standing beside the table, her sleeves rolled up and her arms floured to the elbow, was a young woman. She wore a white blouse and a business-like apron over something very casual, possibly jeans, and her hair was long, darkly curling and happily dishevelled. She seemed please, but not surprised, to see me.

"Oh good!" she said, "You're just in time. Would you prefer tea or coffee, and shall we have it outside or inside?"

I said I would love some tea, and outside please as it was such a lovely day.

The young woman placed cups and saucers on a tray, arranged some of the cakes on a dish and poured tea from a large brown teapot. Then she carried the tray out of the French windows into a conservatory where white wrought-iron garden chairs were arranged around matching tables. Putting her tray on the nearest, she motioned me to a chair and sat down. Then she produced a notepad and pen and regarded me expectantly.

"Right," she began, "What's it all about?"

I was tearfully beginning to stammer my tale when she said quickly "Oh, before you begin, you can stop worrying about John. He's going to be taken care of. Now, let's make a list. What exactly have you got to do today?" and her hand hovered over the paper, ready to begin writing.

At that point the telephone rang beside my bed, dragging me abruptly from the cottage back to real life. The call was from the friend who was coming for lunch. She was dreadfully sorry, but she couldn't make it today. Could we arrange it another time? I said oh dear, and yes of course, and carefully replaced the phone.

I had one whole, unexpected and blissful day free - more than enough for all I had to do with even time to spare.

There was no doubt in my mind that the young woman was Mary, and she had, with efficiency and speed, just turned up trumps.

"She's done me proud on this," I said to myself, "so I shall trust her with everything else", and for the rest of the day and throughout the whole weekend I refused at all costs to think about John and his rate demand. Every time the image obtruded I swept it out again. Mary had sorted out my timetable in one brilliant move. I proposed to leave the rest with her.

On Monday afternoon John phoned. He was laughing. "Something really extraordinary has just happened," he said. "The landlord has just been round. He says if I move into one of his bedsitters by the weekend he'll not only help move my stuff but he'll pay the £280".

I think I shrieked. I certainly felt like it. Anyway, I asked why the landlord was doing this. "He wants to sell the flat," John said, "and wants to do it up".

By the weekend he was installed in a room high on the top floor of a small Victorian terraced house, with a newly scrubbed (by him) bit of ancient vinyl by the cooker, his television set and two new little pot plants. Oh yes, and with that final blessing, a coin-in-the-slot electricity meter! I went for coffee and sat in the window, thinking with amazement of bedsitters appearing out of nowhere, and meters and paid rate demands.

At this point John announced that he was thinking of catching up on his education, which a slight difference of opinion with the headmaster of his Christian-Brother-run grammar school had brought to an unwontedly speedy end half way through his sixth year. "I'm enrolling at South Bristol Tech," he said, "to take my A levels".

Trying not to look too much like the over-zealous, smothering parent (which I have always found to have the opposite effect from the one desired), I agreed this was a good move. At the age of 26, therefore, he returned to student life, passed his A levels with an A and a B and took himself off, together with what seemed to us like ten thousand dizzy teenagers, to Goldsmith College, London University. In due course he left with a First Class Honours degree, and along the way met the girl who was to share his life for some years.

From my very first visit to Mary's cottage, John's life had changed direction. He had, as she promised, been taken care of. So it will not come as any great surprise to find that I returned to that cottage not once but many, many times, and began a kind of continuing unfolding commentary not only of my own personal life but occasionally of other peoples' too.

The next visit, though, was not until more than a week later, which, looking back, I find surprising since after such personal proof I obviously believed in it. But it wasn't until I was thoroughly over-anxious that I consciously took myself back to the garden path and the open door. This time I went into the little parlour and explained that John was living at the very top of a tall building with no fire escape.

"He's a heavy smoker," I bleated, "He'll burn himself to death".

She listened sympathetically. Then she smiled and pointed to the open doorway, in which stood an enormous angel with his arms folded across a massive chest. He had curly hair. "This," she told me "is Rufus, and he's John's guardian angel"

I gazed at this apparition with awe. "He must have given you a terrible time." I said.

Rufus smiled down at me from a great height. "Nothing we can't handle." he replied. So I stopped worrying about John burning himself to death. In fact, for the most part, I stopped worrying about him at all.

After that there was no stopping the visits, and seemingly no end to their consequences. Little by little the scenery opened out and I saw more and more of both cottage and garden.

At first we, Mary and I that is, sat in the conservatory. Sometimes we were alone, but Jesus was present with us more and more and sometimes we were surrounded by angels – mine and others whom I knew to have specific jobs of their own. One of them seemed to be a sort of secretary angel, and very efficient I thought he was, too. My own was already familiar to me and for some reason, for which I have no explanation at all, I had always called him Clive. I know him now as Luke, but for years I didn't seem able to change from the ordinary, if not banal, name I'd given him to one more suitably angelic. Not that he minded. Clive-Luke has always had a marked sense of humour.

For the most part Mary, Jesus, the angels and me would sit discussing problems around a table in the conservatory, and slowly the vista from its glass walls rolled into view, rather like a landscape covered in an early morning mist gradually revealing itself as the day goes on.

One side of the conservatory's glass walls could be opened on runners like a sliding door, and one day I found myself sitting on the grass outside it, feeling the sun on my face and a breeze in my hair. I was alone, but I knew everyone was nearby, within reach if I should need them. In front of me the meadow grass sloped away, down to a deep chasm or narrow valley which I couldn't see from where I sat. Rising up on the other side, facing me, was another sizeable hill, a little bigger than the one I was sitting on. It was covered in brush and trees and rocks. It looked climbable but difficult, and its flat top extended far to my left and out of sight. Its right side sloped downwards in a steep gradient, swooping low to ground level just ahead of me. Its base was hidden by the chasm almost at my feet. Further to the right, the landscape was still misty and invisible.

As I watched this hill, one or two climbers could be seen at various points on its lower slopes, moving slowly and carefully through the brush. One of them stood on a rock, looking around him as if unsure whether to go up or down. It was my husband.

Later, as the hill grew more familiar, I walked around to the left of the cottage and found a cliff top. It was very high and grassy, with the sea sparkling and magnificent stretching to the horizon. This was my own space, a place of special peace, a personal delight where soft breezes from the sea lifted my hair and touched my face and brought the sharp, clean smell of seaweed. I never wore shoes, and the grass between my toes was fresh and crisp. Seagulls cried from the rocks. Everything was delicious, fresh and clean and sweet-smelling, and there was a small stream burbling and bustling on its own splashy way to the sea below. When I was tired or depressed, I let the bubbly water play over my feet.

The freshness of this place was, still is, beyond my power to describe. I knew it to be the freshness of heaven, the freshness of true beauty and the freshness of God. And I decided that the word 'holiness' had been distorted and misused until its only meaning in the world was one of kill-joy piety, a hands-together, mouth-pursed, eye-lowered solemnity which is as far from God as anything could possibly be.

Holiness, I realised, meant a living freshness. The crispness of lettuce straight from the ground, the sweetness of new peas, the smell of wallflowers and honeysuckle and newly mown grass. The warm sharpness of the oranges we picked in Jericho when our mouths filled with juice at the very first bite. Holiness was, I saw, more than just freshness. It was a total absence of decay. Nothing stale could exist in it, and while I wondered for a time how this could be, since everything in life begins fresh but inevitably ends in staleness and old age, I finally understood that in its very paradox lay the reality of eternity.

Outside our material existence there is no Time. God and heaven, being timeless, are in a perpetual *now*. The absolute point of perfection. Humour and wonder and kindness, and the sort of awe which makes us stare at sunsets, and small children flying kites with their grandfathers, and the pattern of sounds in the ether which is the melody and harmony of music – and of course love, love and always love - all these too are simply the non-tangible, non-provable aspects of the same eternity. They, too, are the essence of freshness - and holiness!

On this cliff delicious things happened to me. There I sat with Clive-Luke gazing at the everlasting sea in its dark, sombre moods or in its serene grey-blueness with swathes of purple and turquoise and dancing, shimmering dots. It was a place to retire to in moments of doubt or fatigue, and nobody but me (and of course Clive-Luke, Jesus and his mother) ever went there.

It was absolutely and unquestionably my place.

But one day I discovered that the landscape facing the conservatory had become visible. To the right of the hill opposite there was a flat valley, a plain leading across scrubland to a range of mountains in the distance. One or two of the mountains stood a little in front of the others and one in particular was noticeably different. It was almost entirely conical in shape, a tall pointed triangle over the peak of which shone a brilliant light. And wandering across the scrubland, occasionally disappearing behind rocks and trees, was a path.

I understood that the path was mine to take and that, if I agreed, the conical mountain was my destination.

At the time I was befriending a young man called Jonathon who had been, and still was, severely ill. My praying friends and I had been besieging God for months on his behalf, but recently I had backed away from the problem - temporarily, I supposed, but necessarily since he had become a sizeable and extremely weighty burden and I had plenty of those myself without adding more.

Since my route was obviously going to take me in a new direction, I cast a distinctly curious eye over the terrain and saw my friend climbing the hill to the left, unaware of, or maybe indifferent to, the fact that we'd now be following different paths. I was hardly surprised, but all the same a trifle anxious. He wasn't well enough yet to be branching out on his own. But I told myself he would be fine, he didn't need me any more and I was free to venture off to the triangular mountain with the bright glow at its top.

At that moment I was wafted up into the sky and I could see hill, plain and mountains all laid out below like a map. And I saw that along the top of Jonathon's hill, invisible from the conservatory, was a pathway leading towards the slope and sharply down the far side to meet my own at the bottom. He was making his way along it. I fell asleep that night knowing that whether either of us liked it or not, Jonathon was going to cross my path again.

I had mixed feelings about this. Did I or did I not want to pick up the burden I had just put down? Yes or no? On the whole I thought no. But then, drifting off to sleep, I decided I'd made the whole thing up anyway.

"It's your subconscious," I told myself firmly, "Take no notice".

A few months later I woke with the strongest urge to visit Jonathon and see how he was. I ignored it. Who was I to force help where it wasn't wanted, or even needed? But over the next half hour the urge grew so strong that I asked God what he was playing at. I told him that if it was His idea I wasn't going to comply.

"Don't ask me," I complained. "I've had enough".

But something or someone kept prodding me all the same, so I said "Look, I don't know if it's you telling me, but if it is will you please make it absolutely clear that it's you, so I can't possibly misunderstand?"

Half an hour later the telephone rang. At this stage in my working life, with retirement only a few years away, I had retraced my career steps and gone back to being a library assistant, albeit only a part time one. The assistant in charge of relief staff for branch libraries was asking if I could possibly work that evening. It was officially my day off, but I asked where the branch was. The name was unfamiliar, and it occurred to me that if I could work during the crucial hours it would be impossible to call on Jonathon and I would be safe. So I agreed.

The library was in an area of Bristol that I didn't know, so, having agreed and put the phone down, I looked it up on my A-Z guide. I found that although it was several miles from Jonathon's home, to get there I would have to turn right at a cross-roads where his road turned left - a mere 20-30 yards from his house!

This was a shock, but since by that time it was too late to change my mind, I drove resolutely past and spent an uncomfortable evening in a strange library knowing I must drive straight towards him on my way home again. And when the library closed and I headed for the cross-roads again, there I was staring directly into his side road, almost at his very door.

I stared reproachfully back and knew I was beaten. I had asked for an unmistakable signal and there it was. I parked beside the house and rang the bell. Jonathon answered. He was in his dressing gown and looked terrible, very white with dark, dead eyes.

"How did you know?" he asked.

"I didn't," I replied, "I was told to come so I came".

He was bemused. He sat in his chair in a kind of catatonic stillness, worse than I had seen him for a long time and almost incapable of speech. But I was reluctant to push myself where I wasn't wanted, so I asked if I should stay. He said please, and would I come again - tomorrow if possible. As we talked he grew lighter and lighter. I watched him come back to life like someone waking slowly from a coma, and stayed until he was coherent again. But he was too ill. He had to be hospitalised, which in turn left him homeless. This made him suicidal and at his third attempt he almost succeeded. I watched beside his bed in the Intensive Care unit and during the whole of that day saw him come slowly back from the brink. When the psychiatric hospital finally decided he was fit enough to leave, I found him a bedsitter, encouraged him to pick up the threads of his old life and kept a close eye on him until he was independent again. It took him a full year to recover.

He is now well, active and happy, and has been for years, with a partner and step children and a successful career. No-one will ever really know how much my unexpected visit, with all its dramatic or banal consequences (and there were many of them, believe me!), contributed to his recovery. But I do have to admit that once again God had taken a hand by forcing my own. And it very positively reinforced my belief in the cottage and the view. It had been easy, until then, to forget its beginnings with John and the £280 rate demand, and to regard the whole thing as a pleasant fantasy created by my subconscious for my own amusement out of my own imagination.

Not any more. I now began to take it all very seriously indeed.

CHAPTER ELEVEN

Meanwhile things had been moving quite speedily in a new direction and I found myself unexpectedly (and with the greatest possible reluctance) hurled into another new adventure. I suppose I shouldn't have been surprised. Practically everything I had done in my adult life until then (apart from giving birth to two sons, which was absolutely and totally intentional) had been the result of arm-twisting somewhere along the line..

I became a *bone fide* politician. Almost overnight.

Politics is an alien world. I had been flirting on the edge of it for some years, ever since I had paused one day to actually read the words on the pre-election leaflets dropping through our door. To my surprise I found I had been a Liberal Democrat for years without knowing it. So I hitched my wagon to this new star, and did my share of pushing paper through letterboxes and standing on doorsteps with canvass cards.

Apparently this worked, because one of our candidates for the local elections actually won the seat - not an everyday occurrence at the time, believe me! A few days later the local ward group held a meeting to celebrate and to plan future progress. The next election was two years away, but meanwhile they needed a name to go on their regular Focus newsletters - "to give people someone to identify with…" was the explanation. My husband was with me at the time and, as I was to discover later, Geoffrey preferred being the power behind the throne. I therefore found myself offering to be 'the name', just so long as it was only a 'name' and nothing more because I had no intention - *absolutely* no intention - of ever being a councillor myself. No thanks, I had books to write.

On the way home I just knew without any doubt at all, *ever*, that I had done the wrong thing - and said so. "Oh, it'll be fun," my husband replied reassuringly, "And I doubt if you'd get in anyway. Liberals aren't often elected".

Two months later, the sitting councillor for the ward was pronounced terminally ill and resigned. There was to be a by-election. My name had been proclaimed to the world, my face was plastered on all the leaflets and I was now the candidate.

Since vanity and self respect were involved here, I felt obliged to throw all my energy into the campaign. Electioneering had always been the fun part of politics for me anyway and now that the candidate was actually myself, it became even more exciting and challenging. Just so long as I wasn't actually elected, of course. (My aim was to lose by one vote).

It isn't difficult to guess what happened next. I duly attended the vote count at the local school hall, proudly sporting my extra large orange rosette (as befitted the candidate), and watched while the votes piled up.

To my utter and paralyzing horror, I won. By a comfortable majority. My victory speech was delivered while I was still in a coma from shock and I have no clear idea of what I said - only that I apparently thanked all the right people for the right things in the right sort of way. We all drove off to the Council House in the city, where I was hugged and congratulated and met the other five Liberal Democratic councillors already in place. Then I went home, to be congratulated and hugged again - by the very people who knew I hadn't wanted to win. This puzzled me at the time. It still does. Hadn't they been listening?

Next morning I woke early, to sit in my favourite chair in the dining room gazing out into the garden. I was filled with an icy, horrified despair. What had I done? Why had I allowed myself - *again* - to be persuaded into something I had most definitely not wanted to do?

The next three years were filled with either excitement or boredom or sheer, unadulterated terror – a very tiring combination. Because there were only six of us at the time, the controlling party thought it would be a good idea to exhaust us by putting us on all the committees, and as these all had subcommittees attached, and since I was the only member of our group with no 'day job', I found myself on three of the largest – with, of course, the most sub committees. I was also made party whip.

Speaking personally, I cannot think of a less likely candidate for 'whip' than me, since I can't tell a lie without my nose turning green - but our leader assured me that, far from being a disadvantage, this would work in my favour as no-one would expect me to tell the truth, (the idea being to abstract as much information from the opposition as possible without giving anything away oneself). Since I am also incapable of disciplining anyone over the age of about ten (and then only in ones and twos) my career in the party seemed destined to fail.

Our leader, however, turned out to be correct. The other two party whips were extremely kind to me and even slipped me bits of information I might not have had otherwise. I think I must have been a novelty because we all got on extremely well. As for persuading five highly individual young men to toe the line and agree, I simply used love and persuasion - a matter of necessity in my case. I may have been Whip by name but was in no way Whip by nature and didn't have much choice.

The best part of that role though, was being invited to all the banquets and receptions, in full evening dress of course (my wardrobe thereby expanding itself in the most delightful manner). There were the trips with the other leaders and whips to Germany for Good Relations-type weekends (of which I understand one word in 2,000) and to London to inspect the new light railway; solemn processions through the town and into St Mary Redcliffe church wearing a long fur-edged robe and a three-cornered hat; firework displays seen ring-side from the deck of HMS Bristol. Then there was free parking on the Council House ramp and the use of all the facilities in the Members Services secretarial department; the pleasure of walking the elegant corridors of power and enjoying the beauty of panelled committee rooms – not forgetting the seductively comfortable leather armchairs in the members' common room. All these were experiences I would have missed, advantages I would not otherwise have had. I was even, for a few weeks, voted in by my party members as the new Lord Mayor, being quietly groomed for the part by the City Clerk and the Lord Mayor's Secretary. A last- minute rebellion by the Labour councillors, however, only weeks from hand-over day and against an explicit directive from their local Labour party, eventually put paid to my seductive dreams of grandeur.

I may not have been the world's best councillor, but I would have enjoyed being Lord Mayor (those were the days of living in the Mansion House flat and being transported to functions in the horse-drawn state carriage). But God and the Labour Party disposed otherwise. I can't say I blame them. As chairman of full council meetings I would have made an excellent carpet, notwithstanding the efforts of the City Clerk to guard and defend me!

Unfortunately, three years of trying to grow an extra skin, plus the constant political blood-letting rampant in the council at the time (not to mention the constant misreporting of my words in the press) did for me in the end. A nervous breakdown forced me to retire early (undefeated, I'm happy to say) - but not before I had made my own small mark in the City's history. Motions to full Council which were carried and put into effect; learning to stand up in public and speak on any subject at a moment's notice; 24-hour availability to constituents, some of whom used blackmail ("If you don't mend my pavements I won't vote for you"!) – but most of all having to stand square, to defend my Christian values against the weight of disapproval or disbelief, and sometimes against outright hostility.

Although the experience exhausted me and left me drained, I was aware through all of it that Jesus had not really abandoned me in this lions' den. He may have catapulted me against my will into an alien political jungle, but he did stay in it with me and I was always conscious of his presence and support. Besides, when the right moment came he winkled me out of it again in the nick of time. I had one year to collect my battered wits before disaster struck.

My marriage disintegrated and my husband married someone else.

The following few years were probably the most difficult in my adult life. But although times were hard, I was not inclined to show the world how hard they were. One of the problems with emotional pain is that it is impossible to share without running into pity (which can be unbearable) or the "Pull yourself together" routine (which merely inspires an urgent desire to give the comforter a good slap). Time and again I felt it would have been easier to have broken a leg or gone down with pneumonia. Then I would have received practical, unembarrassed sympathy and support from everyone, not just the sensible few.

I didn't want people to feel sorry for me. The situation was, I felt, partly my own fault anyway. It takes two to build a relationship and two to knock it down again. Not that I wanted to divorce the man I had lived with for 36 years. I was just sadly aware of all the reasons I had given him for preferring his new wife - and deeply regretted them. What I needed was for people to take the situation into account when I made silly mistakes or lost my temper, or suddenly and unaccountably burst into tears. For the most part I hid the pain under a protective coating of careless cheerfulness, and a surprisingly large number of people were deceived. Some of them probably wrote me off as unfeeling, as if I'd been born with different responses, a sort of emotional freak – or that I simply didn't care, glad the marriage was over..

Close friends weren't so easily deceived, even though my emotions were so mixed and so buried that even I couldn’t have told exactly what they were! Norah, Joan, Cathy, Maryrose and my son John, listened and mopped me up and cooked me nutritious meals, and Maryrose suggested that I write her a long letter every week, writing down everything just as it happened. She may not have been prepared for the weight of A4 typing paper that fell in due course through her letterbox, but she was very good about it. She didn't even complain when the letters arrived not only two or three times a week but fell onto her doormat with a pronounced thump. And writing them was wonderfully therapeutic.

Two years later, when most of trauma seemed to be over, she handed me all the letters in a big ring-binder and I turned them into a full length novel called ‘Late Quartet’. Fictionalising it, keeping the storyline but changing the details so they were unrecognisable, became an extraordinary intellectual challenge – the achieving of which was a notable catharsis. I had faced the problems, recognised them, then used them. They had lost their ferocity.

All through this time I had been visiting the cottage. From it I travelled along the path to the conical mountain which was so clearly marked out for me by the mysterious light at its peak. I didn't go every day. Sometimes a week or two passed before I went back to continue the saga, and always there were new hazards to contend with, or new consolations. And the things that happened in that world managed to mirror in the most astonishing way the things taking place, or ones about to take place, in my own.

Some of these events were more important than others, while some were merely pointers. And I met people on the way, acquaintances who smiled and seemed to invite me onto other paths. I never went with them. The light on my mountain was too strong a draw.

The one real surprise came when I approached it and found the light wasn't on top at all but located somewhere much further away, over more mountains towards another sea. Every step I took led me further from the cottage, and the light became a beacon leading over hills and rocks to this new ocean. It glowed like a sunset over the dark line of the horizon.

This is when, in real life, I went to Medjugorje.

CHAPTER TWELVE

Originally, it had not been my intention to go to Medjugorje, but some months earlier a friend had lent me an audio tape by an American called Wayne Weible who talked about this village in Bosnia where Mary herself had been visiting six children at the same time every day, no matter where they were. He spoke with such conviction that I was curious. Was this mysterious Mary the same person as my Mary in her cottage? The only way to find out was to go and see for myself. My two sisters had been there and returned convinced, but I didn't have enough money for the trip and would have stayed unsure and doubtful if my nun sister Kathleen hadn't offered to pay my fare.

Within weeks I was gone.

Medjugorje was once a very small village in a parish of two Bosnian villages not far from the Southern Croatian border. In 1981 the only people who lived there were peasant farmers tilling their small patches of land and keeping their one cow or goat, but by the time I arrived it was a thriving little town. Mary, the mother of Jesus, whom the local people called Gospa, had been appearing every day to the children and was showing every sign of keeping it up. That had meant the descent upon the disconcerted villagers by millions of pilgrims, all needing beds and meals and rosaries to take home. So plots of farm land had been sold and buildings were under construction all over the place, with bulldozers and diggers and mud, and stalls filled with devotional objects and tee shirts and sunhats lining the two main roads and trickling into most of the little side lanes. These led across fields where a solitary cow or goat, or a scatter of hens, meant the subsistence for an entire family, but visible from most places were the two hills, Podbrdo and Krisevac.

The sudden eruption of commercialism, the bulldozers and the shops draped with tee shirts and statues, should have overcome any spiritual ambience by sheer weight of mud and marketing, but they didn't. There was more to Medjugorje than food and rosaries. And after two days I found whatever it was seeping into me like water into a sponge. Among large crowds I saw and listened to three of the young visionaries. I watched from the open space by the church while the sun spun and danced in the sky and threw off glorious lakes of colour. And I went to Mass twice a day.

That was certainly a clear indication that something special was happening there. Never before, even at the peak of my enthusiasm, had I ever thought of going to Mass more than once in the day. ("You must be joking!") yet now it was something I couldn't possibly miss.

Nobody was joking, at least not about that, and I certainly wasn't for the simple reason that on my very first morning I had come upon an unarguable sign that Medjugorje was very special indeed.

It happened in the courtyard of one of the visionaries. All the way there, walking through early sunshine with a group of pilgrims I'd only met at breakfast time, and following a young Serbian guide, I was having an impatient and, to be honest, a rather one-sided conversation with God. I was telling him I couldn't think of going to confession because my life was now so complicated that explaining it to a strange and probably foreign priest would be not only difficult but impossible. What's more, I didn't propose to try. Yet to be in Medjugorje without confessing my sins was going to be difficult all by itself. There was something about the place. So in the end I stopped arguing and said "Okay, if you really want me to go you'll have to arrange it because I can't. So it's over to you".

Minutes later I stood with the rest of the group waiting for the visionary to appear, looking around at the people with detached curiosity. And there, on some steps on the far side of the courtyard, stood my cousin Peter.

Peter is a priest, and Peter knew all about me.

Neither of us had known the other would be there.

After the interview, when the visionary had left us, Peter and I fell upon each other and walked back to the church together.

"Bring me up to date," he said. "What's been going on?" So I brought him up to date and described my feelings and he asked one or two questions. When I finished he said "Well Mary, you seem to have made a very good confession. Would you like me to give you absolution?"

Once I had recovered from the surprise of having my problem sorted in less than an hour, I said yes and he made the sign of the cross over my head, pronouncing the words of absolution right there in the street. He left Medjugorje next morning and I didn't see him again for a year.

After that I had no doubt at all that Mary was appearing in that place and at that time. Certainly nothing else that week surprised me, not even the irrefutable proof Medjugorje was to give of my cottage view, or that the view was to give to Medjugorje.

Of the two local hills, Podbrdo is the smaller, called the Hill of Apparitions because on one side of it Mary first appeared in 1981. About half way up, facing Krisevac, the taller hill, there is a large cross marking the spot and surrounded by stones and gifts and flowers and petitions. All the way to the top are other crosses, some with place names written across them, but all with flowers and burnt-out vessels and candle holders placed by pilgrims eager to send their prayers skywards in one way or another. To reach the main cross on the site itself, one must climb halfway up and then turn to the right along another footpath. I knew this because we had been taken there a few days earlier by our guide.

On the Thursday morning I went there by myself. I wanted to be alone. This time, though, I missed the turning and climbed all the way to the top, where I sat for the entire afternoon, thinking, praying or just simply looking.

It was a significant day. The end of my marriage. The day of our Decree Nisi. It was also April 23rd, the anniversary of the day in 1978 when God had tapped me on the head and lifted me into a core of beauty.

I had already been given one anniversary present. The group travelling with me from London was not, as it happened, the group I was with officially, but because we had spent time together on the journey, we had become quite friendly. This group was almost entirely Anglican, with two of their own vicars, and on that particular Thursday morning they'd been given permission to hold an Anglican service in the first Apparitions Room behind the altar.

Someone had told me about this and I badly wanted to be there, but as the room is very small and the group more than large enough to fill it, I knew there was no chance for me. So when one of the vicars passed on his way there and beckoned me to come with him, I could hardly believe my luck. But this was my big day, even if it wasn't one of unalloyed joy, so I accepted this unexpected gift and followed the vicar.

Out of the twelve or so people in the room only two of us were RCs, myself and a nun. The Communion service, practically indistinguishable from the Catholic Mass, followed the familiar pattern and the atmosphere was beautiful, peaceful, loving and awe-filled. When the time came for the Eucharist I had no hesitation in accepting the host and chalice, and to my relief the nun did the same.

I left the room afterwards feeling I'd been given a far more meaningful present than simply an invitation to an Anglican Communion service. It had been an extraordinary and highly symbolic gesture by Mary, an astonishing, extra blessing on a day of particular meaning.

In a little room behind a Roman Catholic altar where Mary had appeared to the children during the first few years, on the day of my divorce and the anniversary of my re-conversion, I had participated in an Anglican Eucharist. As I sat on the top of her mountain, more her special place than anywhere, I smiled at her across-the-board ecumenism. She had told us quite specifically that it was man who cut the Church cake - not God? How long was it going to take for us to believe her?

So there I was, sitting on the mountain, praying, thinking and just sitting. I decided to stay there until the time came for the daily apparitions. I wanted to watch the spinning sun from a lofty perch, and alone, instead of from outside the church with hundreds of others.

A sun rotating and pulsating in pools of glorious colour was not, by then, a new experience. I'd already seen it twice, once outside the church and once from a moving bus, but it was a sight I felt I could never tire of, and would have sat there day after day on the mere chance of it. So as the time drew nearer, I hoped to enjoy it once again, and sat with my rosary, calm and comforted and coming to terms with my new role as divorcée.

At precisely the right moment the sun began its gyrations, and I sat gazing at it. It was some time, though, before I began to recognise what I was seeing. The whirling, dancing sun was immediately above a conical, triangular mountain. In the background a range of mountains was dark against the horizon, and to the right, between myself and them, was a flat scrubland plain. From the centre of my vision the other mountain, Krisevac, rose in a slope of about one in four to stretch away horizontally far to my left, and the immediate foreground slid away into a steep chasm.

I was looking at my view. And the light which I had always recognised as my destination was the spinning sun itself.

Mary's cottage was Mary's mountain, and I was sitting on it.

To me this was entirely logical. Where else would Mary's cottage be but on her own hill? And what better day could there be for me to discover (a) the validity of my fantasy journeys and (b) the authenticity of the apparitions themselves? One had proved the other, for otherwise how could I, all those years ago, have seen in my mind precisely what I was looking at now?

I returned home with a rather altered view of things. For a start, I had become more Catholic. The Eucharist had grown to mean more to me than just a piece of bread offered merely as a 'commemoration', and I was no longer happy belonging to any Church that not only ignored Mary but actually viewed her with suspicion. I'd had words to say to Mary-cynics in the past.

"Would you like it if somebody snubbed your mother?" I had asked. "So I don't think Jesus can be too happy when people snub his".

Strangely enough, despite the fact that I hadn't really ‘got on’ with her myself in the past, I had nevertheless always been surprised when other denominations had accused RCs of idolatry (‘Mariolatry?’) because there were statues and pictures of her around the place. Did these people not have photographs of parents or children dotted about their homes, and if a sculptor offered them a bronze figure of a favourite grandchild, would they chuck it in the bin?

Gospa never asks for worship for herself, but only for her son. Every word she ever says asks us to follow Jesus, and as mother and friend and queen of prophets, she is the Woman who disproves forever the ancient myth – so long perpetuated by men both in and out of the Church, that women are inferior beings. Now Gospa was visiting earth to help us at a vital time. She had shown herself to be powerful and loving, radiantly beautiful and flesh-and-blood touchable, capable of both laughter and tears. She had also explained where we were going wrong and how to go about putting things right. I personally felt that to ignore such advice under the circumstances would be idiotic – not to say insane!

Besides, Society's image of Mary had turned out to be nothing at all like the person I had met, so how could I now belong to a community that, at worst viewed her with dislike and suspicion and, at best, offered only a lukewarm bow in passing. So I wrote a letter to the leader of the Fellowship I had just joined, explaining as succinctly as I could what Medjugorje had done for me. I was not less ecumenical than before (How could I be, after Mary's own words?) but was probably more so, believing now that divisions in the Church were less a mistake than a world-wide, world-participating crime. A sin of the first order. 'Divide and Rule' had always been good policy for destruction, and the Church had fallen for it - or rather, fallen victim to it.

But Divide and Rule operates on a personal level too, and the time had come for me to stop parcelling myself out in religious chunks.

I never knew how the Fellowship leader, whom I loved dearly, received my explanations. To some denominations, and to most House Fellowships, to be a Roman Catholic is to belong to a cult and sport horns and a tail, so my leader friend probably wrote me off as lost and has been praying for my soul ever since. I'm sorry if my defection caused him any heartache, however mild, but I hope one day I may be able to explain to him properly just what part Mary has played, and is still playing, not only in my own life but in the destiny of mankind itself.

My return home was also marked by the usual crop of gold rosaries, though only one of them was mine.

Perhaps I should explain. Medjugorje is where Mary is still appearing every day. Because of this, certain small miracles happen - some of them not so small, but all of them like gifts she showers on us 'because she can!', and because she wants to. One of these gifts is the spinning sun, but another is that ordinary, everyday rosaries of ordinary, everyday metal sometimes get changed into gold rosaries on the way home. They have become a sort of trade mark of the pilgrimage.

Not every rosary is transformed, so I wasn't expecting anything to happen to mine, but I had bought two little baby Seven Dolours rosaries, with their three sets of seven beads and silvery metal links. They were both of identical size, weight, colour and shape. Also with my luggage were two proper full-sized rosaries belonging to a friend. As I unpacked at home, they fell out of their little bag onto my bed and they had both changed colour. Furthermore, so had one of my little Seven Dolours. The two had begun their journey home identical. Now they weren't.

I showed them to my ex-husband, who weighed them separately on our sensitive balance scales, and the golden one was heavier than its twin. The metal had apparently changed its composition - an impossibility according to my metallurgist friend Dominic.

My friend Joan had been cautious about the Medjugorje experience all along. When she arrived at my bedsitter bringing bread, milk and other essential supplies, I told my story and showed her the rosaries. She smiled politely and said nothing. I wasn't sure she believed me but felt she was giving her very dear friend the benefit of the doubt. Next day she phoned to ask if she could bring something to show me, as she didn't like to trust her own eyes.

Her own rosary, which had of course stayed at home with her all the time, had been lying in its usual place on her dressing table all night. It too had now changed colour. Not all the links, just here and there in a pattern.

I was probably more amused than she was.

Not everyone is impressed, though, by stories like mine. "So what?" some people ask. "What good does it do? Why does she waste time on gold rosaries and spinning suns when she could be stopping all these wars?"

Such questions miss the point. They completely ignore two vital factors. If God is Love, then Jesus is Love, and his mother must be filled with Love. Mothers are famous for giving children little presents, so why shouldn’t she? Gifts from heaven, though, are more than just gifts. They are evidence beyond dispute than heaven exists. They underline our faith in the invisible and they give us hope.

But the best gift of all is freedom to behave in any way we choose. The most barbaric terrorist may do as he likes on earth because his freedom was given to him for a purpose and, once given, can't be taken away again. He was given free will so he could have a free choice - love God or reject him. Imposing action upon him - or any of us - means taking away our freedom of choice, and if we have no freedom of choice our decision - to love or reject - has no value. Try saying "You have *got* to love me." to a potential partner and see how quickly he or she vanishes.

"That's all very well," you might say, "but what about all these wars?"

Unfortunately, free will has its less appealing side. If some human beings were not willing and able to start wars and keep them going there wouldn't be any fighting. Presidents, prime ministers, generals, power-hungry dictators - all these are totally free to kill, main and plunder, either at second hand with megabombs or with their own shot guns. They are also free to rescue, save, heal and negotiate. The choice is theirs, just as it is ours to be resentful and bitter, or friendly and helpful.

Happily, there's another side to this free will business - God can and does interfere if we ask him specifically. And this is precisely what he wants us to do. He is, in fact, waiting impatiently and wondering what's keeping us.

Life, however, must continue. In April 1990 I was obliged to leave Medjugorje and return to all the little problems of life and work - in short, to pick up my burdens from where I'd left them. Despite a mild sense of anticlimax, though, these weren't as heavy as I'd thought. In the deeper parts of me there was new certainty and a profound peace.

Inexplicably, I didn't visit the cottage again for some time, and even now I don't know why that was. But when I did the prospect was the same as before, of limitless sea with a distant sun on the horizon, only now the land behind had vanished and I was on the sea itself, being bucketed about in a tiny boat among gigantic waves. On either side there were towering walls of water, and I lay wet and shivering with cold and fright, in the bottom of my little boat. I wasn't afraid. In the stern a man stood with an oar, calmly judging the waves and keeping us afloat. Curled up in a trembling heap, all I could see of him were feet and hands, but I knew he was there. In charge. He never spoke.

After a while I felt strong enough to sit up, watching the sea and our progress through it with almost detached interest. One day a big ship came alongside and people hauled me onto the deck. They dried me and gave me warm clothes to wear, and I stood in the prow with ocean stretching around us in all directions. A never-ending horizon with a light above it. A great, wet emptiness.

I was on the boat for a very long time. Every time I returned, there I was again, on deck watching for signs of land. I never went below and there was never anyone with me, yet somehow the feeling was never of loneliness, only a weary impatience to arrive - no matter where.

I see now that the waiting, on a solid, safe deck, was an important factor in the journey. I am an impatient person. Waiting has always been a personal torture, with 'not knowing' the worst part of any problem. I was now living alone for the first time in my life, working part-time in a branch library. I told myself this was good discipline, but one day a chance came for action - so I took it.

On Valentine's Day I took my friend Maryrose's advice and gave myself two presents - a new car and a trip round the world.

CHAPTER THIRTEEN

Although she didn't realise this at the time, both car and cruise were instigated by my friend Maryrose. On February 14th 1991 I was lying in bed alone, in an empty house, feeling very sorry for myself. My former husband had re-married and I'd just moved back into our three-bedroomed, detached house with the intention of selling it. The past year had been spent quite happily in a bedsitter, one of seven in a large, graceful house in Bristol, with all the fun of sharing telephone and bathrooms and late night chats with a group of cheerful and lively young women. This had suited me perfectly at the time, but now I was back in my old home, surrounded by familiar furniture shouting with memories but no company, cheerful or otherwise.

So I rang Maryrose and told her I was fed up because no-one had sent me a Valentine card.

"No, no-one has sent me one either." she said, "Go and buy yourself a Valentine present".

I sifted through the mail scattered across the bed and found a brochure for the cruise ship Canberra. This offered a round-the-world trip for the following New Year at a cost of £5,500.

It just so happened that a few days earlier I had received a cheque for £4,000, half an insurance policy which had just matured and into which both Geoffrey and I had paid. Apart from that I had no money, but the house had recently been valued by an estate agent at £125,000 - quite a high figure for 1991- so I reckoned a cruise for £5,500 could reasonably be taken out of it without being missed. As for time off, I decided a plea for compassionate leave, three months without pay, could well be looked on with sympathy by my superiors at the branch library.

At the same time, my rusty old Peugeot had been making scary knocking noises and was getting worse by the minute. So I rose from my couch, dressed carefully and took self and noisy car first to the nearest travel agent, where I put down £300 deposit on my Canberra cruise eleven months away, and then to the nearest Peugeot dealer, taking care to drive slowly when I got there, to muffle the horrifying sounds which I suspected would lessen the price.

"What will you give me for this?" I asked.

£50, I was told. I said I needed a small saloon with sunroof and radio, and what had they got? They showed me a little blue Metro for £370, which I drove home in triumph.

In one glorious morning I had spent my entire £4,000 windfall and I was very, very happy.

I rang Maryrose. "I've taken your advice," I told her "but I'm afraid I bought myself two presents, not one".

She asked what they were. "A new car and a trip round the world" I said.

She laughed and said she liked my style.

So began a year when there was no time for brooding over empty houses and lost companions, for my library superiors wouldn't hear of my three-month leave of absence and turned me down flat. I decided, however, that if God approved of the cruise, both money and time off would somehow materialise. If He didn't, they wouldn't. Anyway, I knew quite well that a leave of absence was within my rights at the time, since another member of staff had just done the same thing - so as the months went by I continued to press for it. Finally, with only two months to go before the payment-in-full deadline, I took my superior through the trade union to a Grievance Procedure hearing..

He was obliged to meet me, plus the union representative and the Personnel manager, and was forced to climb down. I won my time off, but he never forgave me. From then on I was a Marked Woman.

Money was also a problem because although there were plenty of prospective buyers for my house they steadfastly refused to buy it. For one thing it was a local curiosity, a unique 1930's art deco property which attracted the kind of nosey-parker viewers who invariably gave themselves away by saying "I've always wanted to see what this house was like inside". Worse still, in 1991 the property market had just developed a gigantic hole, through which unusual houses like mine were dropping dismally into limbo. So I rang Geoffrey and asked if I could borrow £5,500, to be repaid at the rate of whatever Bank interest he would be losing.

He said yes, but I could forget the interest. God had definitely smiled.

So in the nick of time the rest of the cruise money was paid, the three months leave had been granted, and I was busy packing. And in due course, against all odds, I stood with hundreds of others on the deck of a huge ship, watching the lights of Southampton vanish into the vast darkness of an empty sea.

The ship was massive, with so many staircases it was impossible not to get lost at least twice a day for the first few weeks. Corridors (or should it be companionways?) were elegant with mahogany panelling, lounges sumptuous with deep chairs for nodding off over library books, and for background music there was the quiet hum and throb of engines, and the ever present swish of the sea against the ship's sides.

I shared a tiny cabin with three other ladies, all strangers to me, as is the way when booking cruises on the cheap, and spent most of my time falling over everyone's luggage. However, since their interests were substantially different from my own our paths rarely crossed, and we really only met at dressing time before dinner. Cheaper cabins didn't in those days sport ensuite facilities, so showers were communal and dotted around the ship, perhaps two per corridor. This meant a hopeful dash with towels and shampoo, and the ladies toilets were places where we all beautified ourselves before appearing in the restaurants in our posh frocks.

The restaurants were things of beauty in themselves - one at the prow (the pointy end) for well-off passengers and the other in the stern (the round end) for the rest of us - and each served meals in two sittings. Stewards in white jackets waited for us to choose from our gilt-embossed menus, and in due course served the pheasant and the veal and the swordfish, and delivered mouth-watering desserts. My own breakfasts and lunches were always taken in the deck café, where I could eat fresh mangoes and hot croissants within sight and sound of the ocean.

Entertainments were not only abundant but extremely varied. It was often hard to decide whether to visit the cinema or enjoy the cabaret or watch the stage show, or even snooze gently to a classical pianist. And my days were spent very happily walking four times around the promenade deck (exactly one mile) before breakfast, swimming in the several pools, reading in a corner somewhere and ballroom dancing every afternoon in the special classes – with still more dancing every evening until midnight in the Bonito ballroom.

Then of course there were the 24 ports to be visited, photographs taken and gifts bought at each one, wonderful marvels to be gaped at and admired and photographed, and strange sights and food and smells to be experienced.

I was so busy, in fact, going through my own personal traumas of the past, coupled with romantic adventures in the present, that we were almost within sight of home before I lay one night on my narrow bunk listening to the breathing and rustlings and stirrings (and snorings) of three sleeping ladies and remembered Mary's cottage. I hadn't neglected God altogether. For the first six weeks a delightful, much-travelled Catholic priest with permanent sea legs said Mass every morning, and for the next six an Anglican priest held daily communion services . I went to them all. Unfortunately most of the other Catholics did not. A handful of us on board went forward with the rest to receive his Eucharist, but for the most part the Catholics who had filled the Neptune saloon every morning were noticeably absent, even from the little prayer meeting specially set up for us. Perhaps seven or eight people, led by the ship's professional pianist, spent fifteen minutes or so reading Bible passages and saying one decade of the rosary. This seemed a sad come-down from the 30 or 40 passengers who had turned up for Mass every day for six weeks. I did wonder now and again how these people spent the hour they'd previously spent in communal prayer. Perhaps, like the priest, they had all jumped ship at Sydney!

I was of course yet again swimming against the tide. After all, though I was perfectly entitled to follow my own rules, who was I to lay down rules for other people? In point of fact, they were obeying the Church's rules while I was not. How far is one permitted to go in open disobedience? Who was right and who was wrong?

The question, I have to confess, didn't trouble me much. If I wanted to break what I considered to be a man-made rule here and there, I felt my intentions were good enough for God to honour them. And I wasn't alone. One two others were doing the same thing, and they weren't necessarily Catholics. A Muslim woman was taking serious risks by being at a communion service at all. She and I had wonderful times comparing our beliefs. They were so nearly the same that our differences hardly seemed to count. Her courage was far greater than mine because she'd been to every service, and such disobedience could have cost her her life. One day she told me someone had given her a rosary and would I mind please explaining what it all meant? So we sat in a ballroom, in comfortable armchairs, drinking coffee and going through all the fifteen Mysteries, while around us ladies placidly knitted or made gem trees or pinafore dresses.

Then two Anglican ladies, a mother and daughter, asked me what had happened to give me such a strong faith, so we sat over more coffee and I told them about the day in 1978. On the last day they gave me a gift with a card saying "with our grateful thanks for sharing with us".

There was a charming French Jew, a pied noir born in Algiers among Arabs and with ancestry and upbringing so mixed that religion had become an open question. His home was in France, his grandchildren were Catholics, and the poor chap didn't know where he was. Not surprisingly he had given up religion altogether, but he always listened to what I had to say, albeit in my pigeon French, though whether he was listening out of interest or merely from a desire to please I couldn't be sure. Maybe my none too firm hold on his language made me so incomprehensible he hadn't understood a word anyway!

Most interesting of all was Francis, a divorced American Catholic. We spent the first few weeks deep in discussions which went on sometimes until four o'clock in the morning. We walked under the stars which were subtly changing night by night, or we stared down into the churning water breaking under the bows, and we touched on philosophy and politics and attitudes to life. And of course on God. In fact we talked about God a great deal of the time. We considered all our questions from every angle and eventually he went to the chaplain. When we met again he was calm. After months of struggle he had sorted himself out.

Sadly we stopped pacing the deck together. We paced it separately instead, and I missed him. We did meet occasionally on board, sometimes by chance on shore, and one Sunday we found ourselves together in a Catholic church in Japan. The building was new and the priest was German. We had to take off our shoes at the door and put on large floppy moccasins, and the prayer books were in four parts - Japanese script, phonetic Japanese, English and Latin. So to my happy satisfaction I not only understood everything, I could join in.

A very tiny, very charming lady slipped up to me before the Mass began, to invite us all to tea afterwards. To what I felt was our combined shame, the rest of our party declined because we'd booked a taxi for return to the ship, and the procuring of it in the first place had been such a farce that they hadn't the stomach to repeat it. My American friend and I, however, opted for the tea and decided not to worry about getting home until the time came. So he and I sat in a small, cosy room behind the church, drinking aromatic tea out of delicate cups and eating cakes made of seaweed. One of our hosts spoke perfect English and we had plenty to ask them, so it wasn't until much later that we were offered a lift to the ship in the English-speaking gentleman's car. "Yah boo! for timidity" I thought. Because the rest of our party had been chicken-hearted they'd missed a wonderful experience and a free lift home.

I lost sight of Francis in the end, and the loss became a minor grief in its own right. Did he truly find his God? Permanently? Is he happier than now than he was? Does he still smoke cigars and drink whisky? And, on a more personal level, has he found someone else ready, willing and able to discuss politics, philosophy and the right way to cook spaghetti? Until four in the morning? With only a night off here and there for sleep? These questions are, of course, unlikely to be answered, but perhaps if he sees this book somewhere he will read it and remember.

Unfortunately, though, Medjugorje and the spinning sun and the hill of apparitions had retreated to the back of my conscious thoughts.

Until that particular night, almost within reach of Southampton, when I lay on my bunk in the dark and found myself standing on the familiar cliff top, not facing the sea as usual but looking towards the front path. And on the other side of the path, where before there had been hollyhocks and lavender, a stretch of water was bringing a large ship into a quayside by the cottage door.

I was in two places at once. I was on the cliff watching the ship, and at the same time I was on the ship's deck gazing with surprise at the familiar garden path and the cliff top which I had made my own.

I had come home - encircling my dream world, journeying from cottage kitchen across the plain and over mountains to the sea, crossing oceans in a cockleshell and being lifted to safety on a liner – returning, in fact, to my starting point. I had also traversed the real world. In the same direction, from West to East, from Barbados to Australasia, from Japan to Singapore and around the coast of Africa to home.

I really, truly, had been on the safety of my big ocean liner.

As the truth dawned I lay staring at the base of the upper bunk, only a few feet from my nose. Why hadn't I thought of this before? Why had I spent almost three months with an obscuring curtain over both inner and outer eyes, not making this glaringly obvious connection?

The answer seemed simple. Body and soul may have been catered for by sunshine and ballrooms and by the daily communion services of one sort or another, but Spirit had been taking a bit of a holiday.

Perhaps, I thought, this was a part of the healing process, too. Spiritual peaks are hard things to stay on. Even Peter, James and John were only on the Mount of Transfiguration for a brief spell. Perhaps I needed a spell of earthiness to give point to the cottage when I finally came back to it. But whatever the reason, the consequences were quite profound.

The cottage became more meaningful than ever. I really had come home.

CHAPTER FOURTEEN

Landing back on the good, solid earth of Bristol was a disconcerting experience. Three months incarceration on a vessel, however large, which floats for most of its time on an apparently limitless expanse of water, induces a peculiar, almost claustrophobic state. One is encapsulated, and the only reality is what happens on board. What goes on on the other side of the globe is so far removed from the daily routine that none of it seems to matter very much. The most soul-wrenching problems of the day are whether there's a washing machine free in the laundry room, or has someone beaten you to the showers again? Politicians can be disgraced, governments can totter and wars can flare up and fizzle away again, but deciding between Chopin nocturnes in the Pacific lounge or jazz in the Ocean room can make or destroy an evening. Or even a night's sleep. The notion, however deeply hidden in one's psyche, that one simply can't step off and catch the next bus home tends to alter one's perspective on life's little quirks. So friendships are made or broken by a word, and loves and hatreds are fed and intensified in the enclosed atmosphere of a society forced in upon itself for better or worse.

I had stepped abroad that liner in a state of raw vulnerability. The original pain might have passed (or be presumed to have passed), for the divorce was now two years old, but the wounds had been covered by the thinnest of thin gauzes. The true state of my emotions had, in fact, been protected from prodding fingers by a splendid piece of self deception. I had told myself I didn't care any more, that I was better, that the worst was over.

My error was brought home to me in no time at all. Within three days of setting out on my epic journey all the cuts and bruises were open to view, and hideously at the mercy of trampling feet. Any trampling feet! Worse still, there were no friendly ears into which to pour my tales of woe, no-one to telephone and often nowhere to hide. Weeping bitter tears isn't easy when people are constantly passing by, or when three pairs of ears in a very small cabin will hear the first, tiniest sniffle!

So there was nothing to do but tell myself the truth. It was painful but excellent. Whether my poor fellow passengers thought it was excellent is a moot point. I seemed to spend a good deal of cruising time weeping, for reasons I couldn't even properly explain to myself, let alone my companions. And because I couldn't explain (for after all, where was the broken leg or the hysterectomy scar?) the companions probably left the ship under the impression that was how I normally spent my time. Whatever the cause, I certainly added enough drops of my own salt water to the earth's quota – a superfluous activity in view of where we were.

There were, however, far more good moments than bad. I wasn't always weeping inexplicable tears. Almost at once a routine was established for all of us which gave wonderful solidarity to the day when everything else about the environment went from change to sameness and back again. From jungle heat and lush smells to unequivocal foreignness, from ritzy, glitzy cities to dramatic beauty, life on board was comfortingly predictable.

Finally, having become thoroughly institutionalised, and after four equator crossings, one international dateline, many ballroom dances and 24 ports and cities under our belts, we all came home again. In my case, however, three months of enforced separation from home and earth and loved ones far away had achieved their purpose. The woman who stepped off the ship in April was quite different from the woman who'd stepped onto it in January. Self sufficiency, self confidence and self knowledge (let alone a certain fluency in the French tongue) were all new-but-healthy little shoots springing up on a battered old persona. At least I had some notion of where and how I'd made a mess of things, which can't be bad!

Not least, I had sampled the glamorous lifestyle and been one of the 'beautiful people' that most people make do with reading about in Hello magazine, and after the first excitement had worn off I'd just found it boring. Real glamour, I learned, does not exist. People are people, no matter how elegant their outfits. And sumptuous carpets and magnificent meals in the soft glow of candelabra are only as agreeable as the person sharing the meals and the glow.

I had eaten quite enough magnificent meals. Simple food with a congenial companion to eat it with was going to be enough from now on. In fact, rather to my surprise, I had become a vegetarian – which nicely took care of the simple food. What it didn't take care of was the congenial companion. I had also become very, very choosey. Any companion of the future would have to measure up to an impossibly high standard.

While funny things might be even funnier, beautiful things more beautiful and sad things just a bit less sad in sympathetic and harmonious company, I was now very aware of all the problems surrounding human relationships. Loneliness might one day loom a bit larger than it did at that moment, and coughs and flu can be dismal if one coughs and sneezes alone - but stepping off the gangway onto Southampton quayside was a very definite starting again. I was an embryo. A tiny, new, green shoot. And I had discovered the true value of independence,.

Nothing would ever be quite the same again.

CHAPTER FIFTEEN

Promptly as I returned to work in my branch library, another side of the cottage picture same into sight. It felt like a consolation. I might become lonely from time to time for a life companion 'with skin on', but less material ones were making their presence felt.

Stepping out of the cottage conservatory and turning right, I could now see a whole new landscape. It was dark and noisome, a panorama of black mountains and black earth, of smoke and ash and cold grimness. Tolkien's Mount Doom. And between this harsh bleakness and the cottage was a chasm spanned by a narrow bridge, just wide enough for one person at a time to cross. The rails were so flimsy and frail-looking that I felt it would be a brave soul who tried to set foot on it. On the cottage side of the bridge were many angels. They seemed to be guarding it.

I stood at the safe end, looking across at the gloomy inhospitable landscape and wondering what it meant. Then one day I was encouraged to step onto the bridge myself and to cross to the dark grey, gritty ash. Where my feet had been some small green shoots and tiny white daisies were springing up.

I didn't stay. Shoots and flowers notwithstanding, this was no place for loitering. But I was always aware of the place, a dark balance to the peace and freshness of my cliff-top meadow perched high above the sea, safely out of sight of the menace to the North. I saw this Mount Doom as Danger, as the worst the world could offer, the uselessness of hatred and violence and bitterness and cold greed. And if God wanted to send me there I was going to need all the angels I could get, with human support thrown in as well. He wasn't, however, saying anything. I did ask, but answer there came none! God, it seems, has a firm way with unwanted questions.

Meanwhile things were happening elsewhere. Obeying a sudden impulse - or was it an urgent summons? - I unexpectedly went back to Medjugorje. This, again, had not been my intention.

It just so happened that I was driving home from the shops one morning when I found myself passing my parish church. It was just ten o'clock, so I slammed on the brakes and went in to Mass. I stayed behind for a few minutes afterwards, to think about life and ask God a few questions, then I wandered out to the porch where two women were discussing the Medjugorje visionary Ivan. He'd been on a foreign tour and stopped at Aylesford Priory, where thousands of people had listened to him and seen the sun spinning over the Priory. I was stricken suddenly with anguished disappointment. I hadn't been there.

"Why didn't I know about it?" I wailed. "I'd have gone".

At that time there was a savage war raging in Bosnia, but the women told me that pilgrims were still going to Medjugorje all the same. The agency Centre for Peace was organising tours there once a month.

Joking, I said, "Oh well, as I've missed Aylesford I'll just have to go back to Medjugorje," and climbed serenely into my car. The drive home was not so serene. Every second of the way, my words seemed to be repeating themselves in my head in the most obtrusive fashion. They were so insistent that I hadn't been home more than half an hour before I was telephoning Centre for Peace and asking if it were true that they really were sending pilgrimages into Bosnia and the thick of the battle.

"Certainly," said the young man at the other end.

"Is there one going in October?"

The young man said there was, so I asked him to pencil me in. I then went on to say that my chances of going were more than slim, they were practically skeletal. "I probably can't get the week off at such short notice, and it will be almost impossible to have that Saturday off as I work one in two and they're difficult to swap".

"Well," he said comfortingly, "If Our Lady wants you to go, you'll go".

Next morning I set about testing his theory. The week in question really had been booked by another member of staff, and that Saturday was indeed a working one. So I sighed with secret relief and told myself that at least I'd made the attempt. Maybe that was all that was required of me.

It wasn't, of course. Half an hour later my colleague came back.

"If you really want that week off," she said, "you can have it. I'm moving house in November and it would suit me better to have the time off then".

I was sincerely grateful, but told her I thought the Saturday would probably prove to be an insurmountable obstacle. The librarian in charge had been listening. "That's all right," she said, "You can swap. I'll ask around and see if anyone is willing".

As no-one ever is willing to choose spending a precious Saturday working while their nearest and dearest are loafing about at home, I had serious doubts about finding a suitable (and hopefully understanding) victim. But after a further half hour the librarian came back with the news that my Saturday was free and I could go.

I received this news with mixed emotions. At that point in time, Bosnia was in the middle of a particularly vicious civil war which most reporters seemed to agree was the bloodiest and vilest they had ever witnessed. The pleasant practice of ethnic cleansing was wiping out whole populations, neighbour was fighting (and in some cases torturing) neighbour, and the Serbian Army apparently had it in for anyone who wasn't a Serb. Only a few months earlier, they had surrounded Medjugorje with tanks, and the women, children and visionaries had been hustled into shelters. The tanks had left again, for no reason anyone could see, but the fighting was still very close and the front line was only ten kilometres away.

Did I really want to travel to this scary place on what seemed to be a mere whim?

I decided that yes, I did. If Gospa wanted me to go, she doubtless had something up her sleeve for me to do - in which case I would not only get there but get back again to do whatever it was. So when friends and family drew in their breath sharply and stared, or gently and hesitantly asked if I really knew what I was doing, I wasn't deflected. They might be shocked and afraid for me. I might even be a bit afraid for myself. But on the whole I knew I would go, and that I would come home safely with a fascinating story to tell.

There were plenty of those already. The only bomb to have landed there had obligingly refused to explode. No-one had actually died in Medjugorje (the only fatality being a dog). The pilot who had flown over the village with instructions to bomb it found all his instruments jammed, so he couldn't. Some of these stories might, of course, be apocryphal, but I fully intended to find out one way or another.

I did. Every single one of them had been authenticated!

I was so convinced I'd be safe that there was very little courage involved in going - and I am not especially brave. In fact, not to put too fine a point on it, I'm a coward of the first order.

Forty of us gathered around the Lufthansa desk at Heathrow. We were given white rosaries and Croatian prayer books and mingled with the cheerful ease of fellow voyagers setting off into the unknown. No-one openly expressed the idea that we were all either exceptionally brave, totally mad or just completely lacking in imagination. We certainly all agreed that Gospa, Mary, Our Lady, the Mother of Jesus, had either asked us or told us to go, so what was there to worry about?

"She'll look after us," was the consensus.

She did. We all came back.

Many things happened to many people on the way, though. The journey was tediously long with a seven hour wait at Zagreb airport where there were neither facilities to use nor comfortable chairs to sit on. But it gave all 40 of us a chance to get acquainted, and I spent time with a Croatian lady travelling from Split, who spoke no English but had a rudimentary sort of guide book. This book entranced me by translating only the most extraordinary questions and answers, which bore no relation whatever to what either of us wanted to talk about. So we laughed and drew pictures and diagrams instead and taught each other simple words.

We ate omelettes in a dimly lit restaurant - the dimness being due less to any attempt at a romantic ambience than to the simple lack of electric power. It may have been difficult to see what we were eating, but we were lucky the lights didn't go out altogether. Eventually we took off once again in a Croatian Boeing 727 in the middle of the night, to be transferred an hour later to an unsophisticated coach for a three-hour drive over the border.

It's a strange experience to doze on a bus, in the dark, knowing that the foreign voices and the shadowy persons flashing torches out there are soldiers who may nor may not be friendly - and that this is a military checkpoint. Were we to be ejected from our seats and made to walk home? Or lined up to be shot? Or simply sent back to the airport?

I am happy to say that none of these nasty things happened, the soldiers were Croatian and friendly and the checkpoints easy to cross. By the time we had passed through three of them I was getting blasé, and drifted happily in and out of sleep until the lights of Medjugorje woke us all up. Then we cheered and congratulated ourselves and wondered where we'd all be staying.

Half the group were dropped off quickly at an hotel near the church, but the rest of us were taken further to a smaller house near to Bjakowici, the next village, where we investigated our rooms and my new room-mate flourished a tiny electric kettle. Tea in bed was the aim. We didn't get any. Our host knocked on our door and told us dinner awaited us in the dining room, so we dressed again and sat at long tables where food we were too tired to eat lay spread before us as a reproach.

It was, after all, four o'clock in the morning.

Now comes the difficult part of this story. How is it possible to describe the peace of a place, part village, part raw town, where empty roadside kiosks and half finished hotels speak of commerce strangled in infancy by war and starvation - where supermarket shelves are innocent of anything except two toilet rolls, old packets of tissues and a few not very new biscuits - where every walk to the church, or through fields to the hills, is accompanied by distant (and sometimes not so distant) gunfire and the crunch of shells?

How can one find words for the love I saw in faces pinched with worry and deprivation? What was it about a place so close to a front line that every man one saw wore combat dress, yet gave out such a sense of deep and lasting safety? How could one spend so much time praying in church or just sitting peacefully on the side of a hill, when only a few miles away so much was happening that was the opposite of both prayer and peace?

Naturally, my own personal week was filled with incident, and not all these incidents were happy ones. Relationships were often tricky. There were people I could talk to happily for hours, learn from and share with, but some others I had to struggle to understand and fight to make myself understood. It was a test I didn't pass with much credit because it brought out things I couldn't reconcile. I was unorthodox, a rebel, and it showed.

There were deep moments and hilarious ones, a birthday party with cake and small gifts, and late night conversations in the dark of our small bedroom. And there were mosquitoes which covered our faces and arms with huge, ugly blotches and were a wonderful cure for vanity.

Our guide this time was a slim and attractive Croatian girl with long blonde hair and a nice taste in skirts and tunics - all made by herself - and our host left every night for the local Army headquarters. He pinpointed all the front line positions for me, so I could explain to our politicians the unacceptable truth of this totally unacceptable war. Later, I wrote to the leaders of all the parties, as well as to the Home Secretary and several other Members of Parliament. Labour and Liberal Democrats replied with long, personal letters. The others sent acknowledgements.

Next time I climbed the Hill of Apparitions I took my camera and a local map. The view to the West was certainly the view from the cottage, a mountain range rising up beyond a plain, with a conical mountain ahead. To the South, to my own cliff-top meadow overlooking the sea, there really was a sea - the Adriatic. Some miles away, of course, but there all the same. And to the right - the North, where my Mount Doom squatted craggy and sulphurous in blackened, smoky ash - was the direct path to Mostar, only ten or so kilometres away, and to the capital Sarajevo. In both, the war raged and atrocities were known and barbarous. The darkness of Mount Doom was really and truly darkness, with the darkness of violence and hatred and cruelty!

Faith in my cottage view had been reinforced, underlined by geographical fact. I had much to be grateful for. Unfortunately I wasn't as grateful as I should have been. Human nature isn't always so tidy.

One day I climbed the taller and craggier mountain of Krisevac in a mood of rebellion, and sat at the top pouring my defiance into the sympathetic ear of a Greek orthodox Australian. This unlikely confidante obviously said the right things because I promptly began to feel better. Yielding to a sudden impulse, I placed current photographs of my two sons on a small shelf at the foot of the giant cross which stands at the very top of the hill and which can be seen from wherever in Medjugorje one happens to be.

"There you are," I said to Jesus and his mother, "I'm leaving them in your care and protection. You know better than I do what needs to be done". Later that afternoon I arrived at the church to find a little knot of people gazing up at the cross and pointing.

"Look," they said, "It's spinning".

Since I was at the time extremely short-sighted I couldn't see this for myself, so when my Australian confidante arrived I asked her what she could see.

It was, she told me, unquestionably spinning. The arms of the cross kept disappearing and reappearing, sometimes slowly but often very fast, like a top.

"Isn't it a nice thought?" she said to me, "that your lads are up there under a spinning cross?"

I really did have much to be grateful for.

Earlier in the week I had been invited into the choir loft for that evening's apparition. I waited with the others for Marija to arrive, gazing down into the rapidly filling church and watching the children on the alter who led the rosary each night - holding the microphone before their small faces when it was their turn and swinging their legs when it wasn't. Their voices were young, light and fresh.

When Marija came she made at once for the corner where Mary appears. I watched her kneel in the dark and wondered at my own presence there.

"How can it be?" I asked myself, "that I am standing here, in this place, at this time? How can I be so lucky?"

Of course I didn't see anything, and strangely, didn't feel very much either. But a girl in my group admitted next day that she had seen a light switched on at the vital moment. Because it was switched off again when Marija stood up, the girl thought it was someone's job to switch on an electric light. It wasn't until afterwards that she learned no light is ever switched on. She had seen what no-one else had seen.

I was jealous. "You have so much to be grateful for," I told myself, but no matter how many times I said it, the jealous feelings were there and stayed there, gratitude flickering like a torch with a flat battery. Then one evening, on the last but one night, I was standing crammed into a pew with a large number of other people in a very full church. It was twenty to seven and time for the apparition.

"I'm jealous" I told Mary.

"You needn't be," she replied. "I've come to talk to you".

The words were clear, a loud, firm thought in my head. I stood transfixed with my eyes closed, listening to words telling me things I can't remember now except that they were loving, comforting and reassuring. I do remember, though, that she promised to come again. "Tomorrow," she said, "I'll talk to you again tomorrow".

When I opened my eyes I was still standing up and everyone else was kneeling down. Not that I cared!

That night I fell asleep with a smile, which was still there when I woke up. At last I was grateful.

There were plenty of incidents. One day I was trying to visit someone who was staying at an hotel on the outskirts of the town. It was raining.

A local downpour in Medjugorje is so solidly wet that standing in it is rather like taking a bath. No part of one's person escapes. I had walked a long way and was thoroughly lost, so I dripped despondently into a small café to ask directions. A young woman was leaning idly against a counter talking to a solitary customer, who sat conversationally at a table but didn't seem to be eating or drinking anything. When I named the hotel they conferred, then gave me directions in terrible English which I only half understood. So I set off again, flapping wetly in baggy waterproof trousers and pulling a drawstring hood low over my face. I didn't get far. The woman from the café had fetched her car and pulled up beside me, opening the door for me to get in. She drove me across the town to the lost hotel, and when I tried to thank her she just said "Pouf! It is pleasure".

There was an elderly man who sold fruit every day from a tractor by the roadside. One day I stopped to buy three apples. He dived for a large bunch of grapes and handed them to me, for nothing. And when I thanked him and began to walk away he ran after me with a jug of water which he proceeded to pour over my grapes. "Eat, eat!" he commanded and waved me on.

Once, during the English Mass, the church doors were open for fresh air and sunshine. The priest was reading the Gospel. A man ran very fast beside the church shouting loudly and unintelligibly what sounded like hoarse and urgent warnings. The priest faltered for a second then read on, and Mass continued peacefully to its conclusion. But for most of it I'd been holding conversations with God. It seemed all too likely that the man was a soldier warning us of imminent attack. Perhaps the tanks were on their way and we would all be taken out and shot - or worse!

"How brave am I really?" I asked myself. I knew the answer to that one. Not brave at all. Yet somehow I'd felt that between them Jesus and Gospa had the thing in hand. At the end of Mass we came out into the sunshine and learned that the man was mentally disturbed and was now being cared for.

I apologised to God for my lack of faith. "I'll try to do better in future." I told him.

There is a chapel of Adoration in Medjugorje where it's possible to spend all day in silent meditation, and there are walks across fields and bits of farmland where goats and a cow or two take little notice of passers by, and where unexpected stalls suddenly materialise around corners, tempting pilgrims with sparse displays of rosaries, statues and tee shirts.

There are crosses on Podbrdo, wooden ones and metal ones, and people who sit there in silence. And small cafes (though not many in 1992) and children who should have been at school but weren't because the threat of sudden fighting had closed them.

Everyone smiled at us. They didn't seem to mind these foreign intruders into their anxiety and grief. I once asked a shopkeeper if they did indeed mind. She threw her arms around me, there and then in the shop, and hugged me tearfully. "No, we love you," she said, "It is good for us to see you here. You encourage us, give us hope".

I came home full of thoughts. Above all I knew I had to tell about where I'd been and what had happened. All of it, the whole story from the beginning.

The time had come, I decided, to explain to a sceptical world that praying was not only easy and vital, it worked!

"Seek ye first the Kingdom of God," we are told, "and all these things will be added unto you".

All what things? There is plenty to choose from.

CHAPTER SIXTEEN

Since this was written many more things have happened, in the world as well as in my own life.

For a start, the war in Bosnia finally came to an end a year or so after my second visit, with Croatia, Serbia and Bosnia now living side by side in relative peace. The beautiful Mostar bridge has been rebuilt and the wars have moved elsewhere - to Iraq, Afghanistan and Israel (to name only three).

Gospa, Mary, the mother of Jesus, is still appearing in Medjugorje, although to only one or two of the visionaries. The rest see her just on their birthdays. All of them are married and most of them are parents in their own right. Each month Gospa leaves a message for the world, and they are often similar in style - urging us to come back to her son and to pray not just with words but with the heart. (in other words, in whichever way suits us best). She explains that God is allowing her to stay with us, to help us, and that when she finally goes away she will leave an indestructible sign on the mountain. The messages invariably end with Gospa thanking us for responding to her call.

As for me, what can I say? To describe the events of the last few years as they should be described would take us into another full-length book, so I shall content myself with bringing the story briefly up to the present time instead.

Bus pass now in hand, I was obliged to retire from work as a public library assistant. This meant I had to sell our lovely three-bedroomed house in Bristol (at a huge and crippling financial loss) and move around North Somerset from bedsitter to flat to flat to flat. Nine times in all! In order to keep eating I applied to a local agency, who found me work as a receptionist, first at a golf club and then in a large local office. But as the only employment I had ever really wanted was to write my own words in my books and my own way, as opposed to other peoples' words in their way, my son John suggested I get myself trained as a journalist so I could earn money by writing while the literary masterpieces were in the process of being born. Deciding his advice made sense, I took myself off to the City of Bristol College and, despite two arthritic hips and a broken elbow, emerged at the other end with a diploma. - plus an award as national Senior Learner of the Year 2002.

I also got a job! With the local newspaper.

Unfortunately, after seven eventful and colourful years, my role as local freelance correspondent and feature writer came to an end. I was leaving the area and moving to another which already had a correspondent of its own. It was also getting in the way of achieving my magnum opus. I already had several of those on my shelves, completed and ready to be launched upon an unsuspecting world, and desperately wanted to achieve some more. There were things I had to say that weren't being said. So the Journalist finally faded *out* while the Author faded *in*, and I retired.

This of course has had financial implications in that I stopped earning money, but since earning money up to then had produced so many tussles with benefit offices, council tax offices and income tax departments (not to mention the accountant's fee for sorting it all out), it turned out to be cheaper in the end to give up and give in.

My ex-husband has remained one of my best friends. In the end, he came to believe that something had happened, was still happening in my life. He married an Anglican and both he and his wife became sidesmen at their local church,

As for spiritual progress, like everything else in the world this has its ups and downs, its highs and lows, and mine is no exception. I moved gradually from prayer groups to meditation and finally to private prayer, and from church to church, looking for a home and never really finding one. I suppose one could say I was on a major church-hopping spree! Suddenly finding myself to be a village correspondent, however, I settled down to sharing myself between the Catholic Church in the nearest town and the tiny mediaeval Anglican church in the village where I was living.

A move to nearby Portishead, however, sorted out my allegiance. On the first Sunday there I decided to follow my first instincts and try the Catholic church at the top of the hill. The first thing to catch my eye was a large picture of Our Lady of Medjugorje beneath the altar. It was taken down the following week. Had I tried elsewhere first I would have missed it. But I didn't miss it. I had come home. (The fact that the parish priest and the other parishioners were so warmly welcoming helped, too, of course!).

I am still a rebel. I ask too many questions to be anything else. And like the rest of humankind, I constantly (and sometimes disastrously) fall short of my own standards, let alone God's. But through it all, in spite of it all (possibly because of it all) I've never stopped being aware of the astounding, staggering power of prayer, and the even more staggering, even more powerful love of a personal God who knows our every wish, forgives our peccadilloes and actually wants to *spend time with us.*

All this begs a few questions. Why did that day in 1978 have such a spectacular and lasting effect? The answer is easy - God called and I quite simply fell in love. And when one is in love one wants to stand on the rooftops and shout it to the world. As for that first brief but exhilarating time when miracles were an everyday affair, I had merely taken a leaf out of St Peter's book, leapt out of the boat and for a few wonderful months walked on water.

Of course, like St Peter, I made the mistake of looking down, and realised I was walking in the equivalent of a force ten hurricane - but it didn't matter because a strong arm hauled me up again - and has kept on hauling me up ever since. I've swallowed gallons of water, nearly drowned a few times and every now and again I try to get back in the boat where everything is nice and safe.

It has all been quite a journey, but despite missed signposts, traffic hold-ups, map-reading errors and the occasional road rage (and plenty of mixed metaphors), experience has taught me that everything, absolutely everything, comes down to one word - trust. And trust *works*!

There are a thousand million like me, and there will be a thousand million more, who have made the astonishing discovery that contacting God is astoundingly easy. No telephone, email address or website is necessary. A thought is enough. A wish. The tiniest wisp of a hope. And the truth will dawn that far from only coming when we call, *he has been with us all along.*

Unfortunately too many people have either never been told this truth or don't believe it. I believe the time has come to share it.

"Here I am. I stand at the door and knock. If anyone hears my voice and opens the door I will come in to him and will dine with him, and he with me"

(Revelation 3:20)

Lord, you love me.
You stand at the door and knock.
Give me the courage
To open the door to you
And your life-giving spirit.
Open wide my heart
To share your love
Through patience,
Tolerance and friendship.
Amen

(Sion Community Mission Prayer
Composed April 2007 by St Joseph's
Parish, Portishead)

Set me as a seal upon your heart,
As a seal upon your arm,
For love is as strong as death
Jealousy as cruel as the grave.
Its flames are flames of fire
A most vehement fire.

Many waters cannot quench love
Nor can the floods drown it.
If a man would give for love
All the wealth of his house
It would be utterly despised.

(Song of Solomon Chap 8: 6-7)

Lightning Source UK Ltd.
Milton Keynes UK
09 November 2010

162608UK00002B/15/P

9 781449 033187